Judgment

Series

in

Spiritual

Science

Judgment Series

in

Spiritual Science

Emma Curtis Hopkins

W

WISEWOMAN PRESS

Judgment Series in Spiritual Science

By Emma Curtis Hopkins

Managing Editor: Michael Terranova

ISBN: 978-0-945385-16-5

WiseWoman Press
Portland, OR 97217

www.wisewomanpress.com

Acknowledgements

The editors at WiseWoman Press wish to acknowledge the efforts of Rev. Joanna Rogers and Rev. Marge Flotron, and the members of the High Watch Fellowship, who kept this work available to the determined student over the past century.

Editor's Note

The various versions of this text printed over the past century used a spelling of the word "judgment" that included an extra "e"—as in "judgement." Since modern usage and text editors do not recognize this spelling,, we have used the modern version throughout this publication.

Also, because the author didn't often explain her references, we have attempted to do so, using footnotes to provide the information that she assumed her students already had.

Foreword

By Rev. Michael Terranova,

Emma Curtis Hopkins was one of the greatest influences on the New Thought movement. She taught over 50,000 people her method of knowing that God is all there is. She taught the founders of all the New Thought organizations around today, or her students taught them. All her writings are geared to help the student or reader let go of anything except the one Presence. She presses us to deny anything except the Truth of that spiritual Presence we call God, and to affirm only that Presence as all there is.

Not much is known about her personal history as she was a very private person. What we do know is gleaned from other peoples' memories and stories, or from the archived writings we have been able to discover. She was born in 1849 on a farm outside of Killingsly, Connecticut, and passed on in the spring of 1925. She had a marvelous education and could read many of the classical texts in their own language. She found the Truth in all the religions she studied. She quotes all these teachings in her writings.

Still, Emma uses Jesus Christ as the main example in all her works and classes. Her use of bible quotes is one of her main ways to support her beliefs and teachings.

Emma coined the words Religious Science, Divine Science, and others that are used even today. Her works after the middle 1890s often use the word Science with various qualifiers. The word Science was prevalent in most of the metaphysical writings in the middle and late 1800s, as well as today. In the late 1800s all metaphysical study of healing was called Christian Science, a term developed by Phineas Quimby around 1850, until Mary Baker Eddy won the sole right to use the name. There were many names used after that. Many metaphysical organizations still use the word Science in their teachings.

Emma is really clear that matter is not the Reality of God. She expands on Mary Baker Eddy's premise that God is the only reality and everything else is what there would be if God were not all. This concept is one of the hardest to really grasp as we live in the physical world and have a hard time believing this is not the true Reality.

Her writings are written in a poetic form and have a Victorian flavor. She uses many examples of demonstrations that have been experienced by historical figures, many of whom we do not know much about, today. She also uses many examples of the physical sciences of the day to convey her teachings and prove God is all there is.

Emma seldom named the source of her quotes and never used footnotes. She figured everyone knew the people and incidents she quoted. There are fewer of these in the *Judgment Series,* making this one of the easiest books of Emma's teachings to understand. It seems like it was written at a level most people can understand. This is also the only book in which she tells the reader which books contain her basic teachings and which ones have the deeper teachings. She says her deeper teachings are in *Esoteric Philosophy* (WiseWoman Press will be publishing *Esoteric Philosophy* in the near future.)

All of Emma's teachings are presented in 12 chapters, or lessons. Her first six lessons always deal with the human personality or ego. The last six lessons always deal with expressing in the world. The first chapter is always "The Thing Itself," or God as all there is. The second chapter has to do with denying anything that is not the Truth of God. The third is affirming the Truth. Each succeeding chapter expands on the Truth that God is all. Her progression in the lessons is designed to have us train our personal mind to be the one with the universal Mind of God.

It is very hard to discern if the works attributed to her were actually written by her. Shorthand was widely used in the late 1800s and early 1900s, and many lecturers arranged for people to take down what they were saying, so most of the works we have may have been transcribed as she taught different classes. *High Mysticism* and *Re-sumé* were most likely her own writings, since she kept updating them until the early 1900s. She also wrote bible interpretation articles for the <u>Chicago Inter-Ocean News</u>, (which WiseWoman Press is in the process for collecting for future publication). These are the only other writings we can be sure were actually hers.

Each of her works is aimed at a different depth of understanding. The *Judgment Series* seems to be geared to understanding what she is teaching at the mental level. It is one of the easiest of her works to understand and to follow her particular line of reasoning. This book has never been in wide circulation and it is my hope it will open the door for more students to grasp her teachings.

May this book open you to a new understanding of the Truth that God is all there is and that, as she states, "there is Good for me and I ought to have it."

June, 2008
Emma Curtis Hopkins Center of Vancouver, Washington
www.emmacurtishopkins.net

CONTENTS

Foreword..i

I. THE WORD..1

    "In the beginning, God." [Genesis 1:11]..1

II. DENIAL..11

    "God said: Let there be Light." [Genesis 1:3]..11

III. AFFIRMATION..21

    "And God saw the Light that it was good." [Genesis 1:4]..........................21

    "God is able of these stones to raise up children unto Abraham." [Luke 3:8]21

    "And the third angel sounded and there fell a great star from heaven, burning
    as it were a lamp, and it fell upon the third part of the rivers, and upon the
    fountains of waters; and the name of the star is called wormwood."
    [Revelation 8:10] 21

IV. FAITH 33

    "And God said. Let there be a firmament in the midst of the waters." [Genesis
    1:6]..33

    "And the fourth angel sounded and the third part of the sun was smitten, and
    the third part of the moon, and the third part of the stars, so as the third part
    of them was darkened, and the day shone not for the third part of it, and the
    night likewise. And I beheld, and heard an angel flying through the midst of
    heaven saying with a loud voice. Woe, woe, woe, to the inhabitants of the
    earth by reason of the other voices of the trumpets of the three angels which
    are yet to sound." [Revelation 8:12-13] 33

V. WORKS...45

    "And God said, let the waters be gathered together in one place and let the
    dry land appear." [Genesis 1 :9] 45

    "And the fifth angel sounded, and I saw a star fall from heaven unto the
    earth, and to him was given the key of the bottomless pit." [Revelation 9:1]45

VI. UNDERSTANDING..59

    "And God saw that it was good." [Genesis 1:10] 59

    "And the sixth angel sounded, and I heard a voice from the four horns of the
    golden altar which is before God, saying to the sixth angel which had the
    trumpet. Loose the four angels which are bound in the great river Euphrates."
    [Revelation 9:13-14]..59

    "And it shall come to pass in that day, I will hear, saith the Lord. I will hear
    the heavens, and they shall hear the earth." [Hosea 2:21] 59

    "O Lord, I beseech thee, send now prosperity. Blessed be he that cometh in
    the Name of the Lord. We have blessed you out of the house of the Lord."
    [Psalms 118:25-26]..59

VII. INHERITANCE 73

"And god said. Let the earth bring forth grass, the herb yielding seed, and the fruit tree yielding fruit, after its kind, whose seed is in itself." [Genesis 1:1 1]73

"And the seventh angel sounded; and there were great voices in heaven, saying. The kingdoms of this world are become the kingdoms of our Lord, and of His Christ; and He shall reign forever and forever. And the four and twenty elders, which sat before God on their seats, fell upon their faces." [Revelation 1 1:15-16] 73

"Bring forth, therefore, fruits meet for repentance." [Matthew 3:8] 73

VIII. TRUTH.. 87

"And God said. Let there be lights in the firmament of the heavens." [Genesis 1 :14] 87

"And the nations were angry, and thy wrath is come, and the time of the dead, that they should be judged, and that thou shouldst give reward unto thy servants and prophets and to the saints, and them that fear thy Name, small and great; and shouldst destroy them which destroy the earth." [Revelation 11:18] 87

IX. HOLINESS 103

"And God said, Let the waters bring forth abundantly. " [Genesis 1:20].... 103

"And the temple of God was opened in heaven." [Revelation 11:19]......... 103

X. FORGIVENESS.. 113

"And God said: Let the earth bring forth the living creature after his kind, cattle and creeping things." [Genesis 1 :24]... 113

"And the nations were angry, and Thy wrath is come, and the time of the dead that they should be judged, and that THOU shouldst give reward unto thy servants."   [Revelation 11 :18]... 113

XI. WISDOM.. 123

"And God said, Let us make man in our image, after our likeness; and let them have dominion." [Genesis 1 :26] 123

"And the temple of God was opened in heaven and there was seen in his temple the ark of his testament." [Revelation 11:19] 123

"The eleventh a jacinth." [Revelation 21:20] 123

XII. FREE GRACE... 133

"God said unto them, Be fruitful, and multiply and replenish the earth ... And God saw everything that He had made and behold it was very good." [Genesis 1:28-31] 133

"And the seven angels which had the seven trumpets prepared themselves to sound." [Revelation 8 :6]... 133

"And there were voices, and thunderings, and an earthquake, and great hail." [Revelation 8:5].. 133

"And they sing the song of Moses, the servant of God, and the song of the Lamb." [Revelation 15:3].. 133

I

THE WORD

"In the beginning, God..." [Genesis 1:11]

There are three methods of calling attention to what IS.

First: The statement of self-evident principles. This is ethical philosophy, or the metaphysical axioms of Spiritual Science.

Second: The illustrative method. All Bibles, so-called, are illustrative, i.e., are filled with fables of men, women, tribes, families, who are living object lessons of how the metaphysical axioms act when lived out. Jesus, standing silent in the Nazarene temple with all eyes upon Him, represents the eternally young soul dwelling within myself. All my mental and physical gaze is directed towards my soul, but the instant I hear it speak, I run with every faculty alert to hush its voice, exactly as the whole of Nazareth ran to destroy Jesus for speaking of unworldly, unmaterial evidences that mankind should never grow old, as their soul never ages.

Third: The unpremeditated experimental. This is like Berkeley's, Collyer's and Edwards'[1] sudden discovery that things had no objective existence independent of their mind. Even Schopenhauer found that the whole world was his mental presentation. Jesus found Himself able to turn water into wine by changing His thought from water thought to wine thought. Many people have found objects and people regulated by their states of mind and demoralized by new states thereof. The moment I leave the fixed notions I have held in mind, I find new business affairs. If I have been making a success with my mind as it is, I must be sure that the new mind that I think of making up has in it the success qualities also. Change of mind is change of city. Change of mind is change of acquaintanceship. Experiences proved this on some lines to Berkeley, Collyer, Schopenhauer. They did not discover all the ethical principles on their marches, but found experiences confirming all of them that they did discover.

This world is governed by ideas. Jesus Christ said He refused to be governed by ideas. He refused to govern by ideas. "My kingdom is not of this world," He said. He did, however, often use ideas to swing affairs into shape, as when He said, "Lazarus, come forth." He went up on the cross in

---

[1] These philosophers were the "last word" in spiritual philosophy in the early 19th century.

response to the prophetic language which said that it was the way to call the world's attention to His God nature. He was, therefore, obedient to an idea. He governed at times by an idea. But He was not an idea. He was Un-idea-ed Being taking up a bunch of ideas and laying it down at will.

The Bible is a book of axioms and illustrations.

The Soul in me is Jesus Christ. As told in our Bible, that Soul puts on me and takes off me. When I see my Soul I am soon all Soul, just as a child who watches a serpent is soon swallowed in serpent. Serpent is wisdom. Soul is wisdom. The wisdom of Soul is symbolized not by serpent, but by Jesus. The wisdom of the world is serpent wisdom. The wisdom of God is Jesus wisdom. The Soul says, "Look unto me." The world says, "Be thoroughly educated in my methods so as to defeat and overtop your neighbor." Jesus says, "My kingdom is not world ideas."

To know the Soul in myself is what I really am after with all my faculties. The three methods used by all the metaphysicians of the world have for their purpose or object the turning of my faculties backward to look at my Soul, or God nature. All my faculties are in pain or pleasure with their efforts to look back towards the Me from whence they started. Even in looking away from the Soul, all faculties seek their "I."

"Turn ye—turn ye, for why will ye die?" Looking away from the "I" they perish in pain. Looking towards the "I" starting point, they experience neither pleasure nor pain—they are the unbiased, undeceived Soul towards which they look.

The Hindus have been studying mind for many generations. Today they are mental adepts. As ancient Greece was devoted to sculpture; as ancient Egypt was devoted to stupendous buildings; as ancient China was devoted to book learning; as Italy has forever been devoted to music and painting; as Germany has always been devoted to logic—so India, ancient and modern, has no object or aim outside of mental philosophy, or speculative principles put into demonstration.

At the first height of their learning, what have they found out? This, namely, that all the pomp of sea and sky, woods and hills, which the eyes behold, is illusion—an hypnotic experience of the human mind; that all grief and love, and the causes of grief and love, are also hypnotic experiences of the human mind; that all judgment or choice between successful movements and failing enterprises is but a choice between two hypnotic states of mind; that he who shall be able to lay down these pairs of opposites and be himself, is the true one.

Thus, to be the true one is each man's privilege.

By the Bible parables, we are shown a Job to represent one who had exercised no conscious choice for riches, but had been rich; who had exercised no conscious choice to be poor, but was poor. He objected to being whiffled about in such fashions and rose in wrath, grief, will of mind, to hurl off delusions. He found himself. Then, having risen above good winds of prosperity and evil winds of adversity, he wrapped around himself, in full knowledge of what he was doing, an entirely new environment.

In the Bible illustrations, a Jesus is made to represent one who had never been deluded, never hypnotized, never deceived. "He needed not that any man should teach him." He said, "Destroy this temple and in three days I will build it again" [John 2:19]. And "I can lay down this life and I can take it up again" [John 10:18]. He represents the actual powers of the Soul that dwell in every man, woman and child.

He represented the way you and I will do when, instead of being whiffled from our delusive state called trouble and gloom, to the opposite delusive state called pleasure and happiness, we are able to take the ingredients that constitute these and enfold ourselves with either or neither at will. He represented the use of ideas to mold things and events with, and He represented being independent of ideas.

He saw that the world's states are manageable by one who can judge with his mind exactly what thoughts to mix. Did he not stand in a temple and use choice for riches, but had been rich; who had exercised no conscious choice to be poor, but was poor. He objected to being whiffled about in such fashions and rose in wrath, grief, will of mind, to hurl off delusions. He found himself. Then, having risen above good winds of prosperity and evil winds of adversity, he wrapped around himself, in full knowledge of what he was doing, an entirely new environment.

In the Bible illustrations, Jesus is made to represent one who had never been deluded, never hypnotized, never deceived. "He needed not that any man should teach him." He said, "Destroy this temple and in three days I will build it again." [John 2:19] And "I can lay down this life and I can take it up again." [John 10:18] He represents the actual powers of the Soul that dwell in every man, woman and child.

He represented the way you and I will do when, instead of being whiffled from our delusive state called trouble and gloom, to the opposite delusive state called pleasure and happiness, we are able to take the ingredients that constitute these and enfold ourselves with either or neither at will. He represented the use of ideas to mold things and events with, and He represented being independent of ideas.

He saw that the world's states are manageable by one who can judge with his mind exactly what thoughts to mix. Did he not stand in a temple and use to look into this region, to watch it steadily. It lifts all the faculties of mind, sense, body, out of themselves.

"By thine own Soul's law, learn to live, And if men thwart thee, do not heed."

The wise men of all countries have sought to look upon their Soul, their own "I AM." When you find them able to lay down their body and take it up again at will, you may know they have found their own Soul, their Jesus Christ, undescribed, sinless "I AM." When you find them able to turn thoughts from sick thoughts into well thoughts at will, then you may know they have found their own Soul, their Jesus Christ, unhypnotized "I AM." When you find them doing these things, and then not doing them, yet trying to do them, you may know they are still being whiffled in the delusion of pairs of opposites. They have not found their own will.

The Buddhists have 600 million believers because so many of them have almost seen their Soul.

The Muslims have 200 million believers because so many truths have been spoken of each man's own God Soul.

The Christians have 400 million believers because they describe one man who found His own soul; who stood on Hattin Heights[2] and notified the race of men what their rights are and were and forever shall be—not as intellect molding human events with painful struggles, but as Soul, God, shining on whomsoever it will—in whatsoever fashion it will, unhinderable, undefeatable, unspeakable Light.

---

[2] This is usually referred to as the "Sermon on the Mount."

There are six Bibles which bring forward the axiomatic principles of the Soul as man has caught glimpses of it and reported what he has seen, felt, realized. They tell the Truth as far as the intellects of the writers were windows open enough to let Truth be told. Fix upon one of these Bibles at a time, and at the end of the reading of them, choose which one has turned you backward towards your own "I AM" with most powerful pushes. Read that one three times over.

These Bibles are:

Christian Bible

Hindu Bhagavad-Gita

Chinese Tao-te-King

Egyptian Book of the Dead

Mohammedan Al-Koran

Zoroastrian Zend Avesta[3]

Know, however, that no bible is equal to Soul speech.

Spiritual Science means Christ Jesus speaking; or the speech of the Soul in all men, which

---

[3] Mrs. Hopkins added the *Zend-Avesta* to her initial list of the world's major Scriptures in her later writings, increasing it from 5 to 6.

has been called Christ Jesus.[4] It starts out with the statement of the Presence of God everywhere, the Power of God everywhere, the Science God everywhere.

There is no direction in which we can turn but that fronting us is our own Soul, or our own God. There is nothing we can know like knowing God, the Presence, Power, Science, that takes us from sight of delusions to sight of undeluded Soul.

He who sights his own Soul started out by turning to watch that region of him which was not married when he signed his marriage bonds, was not born when he lighted on the globe, and lies not down in the grave when he lieth down. He turned to look at that in him which was not converted when he was turned into the church, and which he has deplored as his unregenerated being, has prayed over, wondered at, feared, snubbed, hated, hidden, but could not manage. He has at last given It its own way, with all his faculties stilled and unpretending. Then he has risen with something like new fires, new truths, new powers.

Often to this Soul he has said: God! God! God!

He has spoken again, God! God! God!

---

[4] Note that she is saying that there is one soul, across humanity, and that it is called Christ Jesus. This is consistent with *A Course in Miracles*, a popular metaphysical text published by the Foundation for Inner Peace since the 1970s. Its narrator refers to himself as Jesus and tells the reader that all of us together make up the Son of God.

Lost in speechless adoration, he has fallen senseless at the sight—one sight—even afar off—of his own Soul. Upon rising, he has looked again, and in adoring humility, all his conscious being has again cried: God! God! God!

Then one Man in one stupendous moment said, Jesus Christ!

And that word answered through Him, saying "Ask in My Name. I AM HE."

II

DENIAL

"God said: Let there be Light." [Genesis 1:3]

Sight of that region in me that was never born, is not now at all interested in my welfare, and will not die when I lie down, will make even my human mind, or ego, indifferent.

Epectitus[5] did not sight his Soul straight, but by speculative philosophy he reasoned about it so well that when his master wrenched his leg to find out how much pain he could bear, he said in calm indifference: "Take care! You will break it." And "There! You have done it!" when it snapped. He had not touched his Soul's indifference to pain and pleasure far enough to feel the power to set the leg again with his will.

---

[5] Epectitus - Greek Stoic philosopher [c. 50-120 AD.] was born a slave in Hierapolis in Phrygia. As a result of his early life, he had a passion for freedom (even in its negative aspects), regarding it as the highest possible good.

"By these signs shall ye know" when ye are my disciples, or are learners from your Soul,

"If I do not the works of the Father, believe me not."

This does not set works above knowledge or sight of God, but it shows that one straight sight of the Soul region confers that working energy.

Reasoning about the Soul confers indifference to power and also confers power.

"Plato, thou reasonest well." What reasoning used he? What power had he? He said the death of the body cannot injure the Soul. His power was in calling to his thoughts the greatest minds of his age. He knew not of molding nature and destiny as his own rightful power. "We look for one to come who shall subdue human passions, nature and destiny," he said. Five hundred years later, the Judean hills felt the tread of this Master on their rocky heights.

Philosophers, religionists, experimentalists have sought for what would subdue nature's heat, cold, tidal waves, old age, death, anger, grief, lust. They have sought for what would master the fate that pursues all men, pushing them into sorrow and prosperity at its own will, while they submitted groaning or smiling. They have looked for Light—Light—Light. Always they have believed the light would give them freedom. This freedom has really been man's lodestone—his pole star—his goal. Thus, when One told the description of how the Soul talks through man when it is free, He had to say, "Ye shall know the Truth and the Truth shall make you free."

If man thinks a thought and believes that thought, it has control over him, insofar as he believes it. He is not then free while that thought compels his mind's belief. If he believes it not, he is free from it. Thus, if I believe that I am healthy, I am in bondage to my belief in health. If I do not believe I am healthy, I am free from health. I have no health. Now, am I swung from believing in health to believing in sickness? Alas! I am in bondage again. This time I do not like my bondage.

Is the bird free because he likes his little brass cage? This is health. Is man free because he is in health? Is not the bird free which can fly in the wide woods or curl into his cage at will? Is not mind a free will if it can fly as a healthy body or curl down in sickness as it pleases? But is a mind free which has an idea that it must bear a sick body or a well body all the time about with it? Is a mind free which feels it a duty it owes to itself or its world to lug about a body whether that body be light or heavy? Is not mind freer when it can lay down its body and feel no obligation whatsoever to pick it up again, than when it can simply make its body sick or well at will?

Thus, He who said He could leave His body forever or assume it at any time unobligated, was free. He represented freedom.

If we are obligated to do or be anything, we are not free. If we are not free, we do not know Truth. If we do not know Truth, we have not seen our Soul. As shadows of posts are lost in posts, so we must be lost in Soul. Lost in Soul we speak Truth. Speaking Truth from the Soul standing, place, we are in the Light.

Light is life, health, happiness. We are not bound to life by believing in life, but life is an easy and light gift with which we have nothing to do. We are not bound to health or happiness by believing in them, but they are free gifts with which mind has nothing to do.

Thus the Soul, when it is represented as Jesus Christ must say: "My yoke is easy."

"The Light is the Life of man" "The Life is the Light of man." The gift of God is eternal life.

There is, therefore, an easier way of living than by believing in health and happiness. It is by having nothing to do with health or happiness, not even in mind. Does God have to believe in happiness in order to be happy? Then, poor God, He is not free! The silence of Jesus Christ is His freedom from obligation to speak. The absence of Jesus Christ is His freedom from obligation to be present. The invisibility of Jesus Christ is His freedom from obligation to show Himself. Thus does the Name, Jesus Christ, truly represent the state of the Soul which knows that no obligations rest upon It. Now, while I am obliged to do anything, I am not in the Light with my mind in any sense of the word. While I am obliged to believe in something in order to keep my mind straight and clear, my mind is not in the Light.

When John, the Revelator spoke of the first angel sounding, he said it caused all nature to be leveled by hail and fire. The first lesson in Spiritual Science will fell every thought man has ever had, to the ground-bed of his mind, where it looks not toward anything going on around, but turns to see its Source. It will spread through the airs round about you with leveling influence for you to even read the lesson in Judgment.

John was speaking of the final day-the end of hypnotic pageantry of sky and sea, woods and hills, men and horses, cattle and money. This was Judgment and the end of Judgment. Judgment is choice. End of Judgment is being above choice.

Notice how people want the money-kings thrown down. Notice how the crowned heads tremble. Notice how people humble their presidents or princes by killing them or voting them out. What did it? Your knowledge that the Soul in peasant and the Soul in Czar is one and the same Soul-no difference. This knowledge has struck the planet a sharp rap. Everything falls. Every low thing feels its equal rights with all things.

The second angel of the Judgment sounded and a mountain of fire disappeared into the sea. What is this mountain of fire? It is your obligation—all obligation. Debt is obligation to do something, think something, or be something.

Obligation solidifies into honorable duty. Honorable duty gets on fire with anxiety. When you feel under obligation to please someone, or do something for their sake, you face the mountain of debt solidified into duty, on fire with anxiety. Before you is a high hiding. Beside you is a high hiding. Behind you is a high hiding. Even though you fall down under the knowledge of the free sky of Soul far above your mountain, yet the second angel of Judgment has not sounded.

Does the Soul have to be and do anything like unto this world's ways? Is not the Soul, God? Alas, poor God, if He, too, is behind a mountain of fire—obligated—in honor bound—anxious.

Twelve points of Truth:

1. That which is true of God is true of man at his God point.

2. That which is not true of God is not true of man at his God point.

3. The God in man is his *reality*—his substance.

4. As God's universe is Himself, so man's universe is himself.

5. As God is, and need do nothing at all to be all, so man is, and needs do nothing to be all.

6. As there is no God over God, so there is no God over man.

7. As God wishes for nothing, having all, so man wants nothing, having all.

8. As God is not deceived, so man at his God point is not deceived.

9. As God sins not, so man at his God point sins not.

10. As God needs no judgment, so man at his God point needs no judgment.

11. As God is Absolute in beauty, freedom and security, so man at his God point is absolute in beauty, freedom and security.

12. As God is all, so man at his God point is all.

We can soon settle any question of our duty by taking note of our God point. If we cannot find our God point, we have only to notice that region of us which is not interested in anything, not even in the highest love of our life, nor the highest religion of our life. It is possible for anyone to take notice of this region.

Hufeland, a Prussian doctor, noticed in some of his patients a region of them, which was not interested in their sickness. Watching that indifferent region himself, he caused them to get well. The mountain of his obligation to cure them fell away into the sea of that Soul in them.

All debts disappear. All duties disappear. All obligations disappear. All anxieties disappear. All matter ceases to exist.

It is no wonder Spiritual Scientists soon found the Truth to be that there is no burden—no matter—no hardship. It is no wonder they were all able to say, "There is no God over me." No wonder

Mahomet (Mohammed) said. "There is no God but God." The *very* first angel crieth, "One." The sound of his voice levels all men to the Soul point.

The Brahmins of old, watching for the Soul point in man, which no eye of flesh can see, said, "It is the infinitely Small One." Then they cried, "All things are lost in the Small One." If the One who is too small to be noticed, too indifferent to be pretentious, too unheralded to find room in the inn of human mind, is to swallow up all things, how wonderful, wonderful is He!

Did the little Jesus find room in the inn when He came to its doors? If Jesus was another Name for Soul, you can see why you have not yourself let Jesus into your notice. But now that the judgment has come, you are glad to dissolve your whole notice into notice of that region of you which has nothing whatsoever to do with your affairs. The breath of freedom as it wafts

Sight of the Soul is light of the Soul, mind of the Soul, speech of the Soul. Sight of the Soul is sight of the I AM.

Moses watched the strange region in his own being for 40 years and then undertook to execute the freedom of the Jews by it. He was defeated. He then watched for 40 other years, and when he again undertook the cause of the Jews, he succeeded. Forty is a period consecrated to watching. Jesus watched 40 days. It is not as we reckon time, but as aloofness from distractions. Moses' first 40 years were mixed with learning, war and court splendors. His second 40 were spent marrying, bringing up children and tending sheep.

Jesus' time was unmixed. It may not have been days, but it was unmixed attention.

The name Moses brings forth attention to what he found out. His soul had so loud a tone to him that it seemed to speak from a flame of fire before his eyes. He asked his Soul's name and it answered: "I am that I am." He heard it promise him that it would do all things for him and he need do nothing.

"Take no thought, saying. What shall we eat?"

He seemed to do all, yet he did nothing. So Jesus seemed to do all, yet He did nothing. "The Father that dwelleth in Me, He doeth the works." So when the Soul of myself calls its name, I, too, may converse face to face. I, too, may do all things yet do nothing.

Hark! My Soul calls! I turn to hear Its voice. "I am not what I am not." "I am not bound to do or be."

This is the way it sounds to me now. All my fiery mountain of care, of anxiety, yea, even of my honorable duties, have faded from sight. The fiery mountain of duty is the last name of those high piled beliefs of mind when it is not taking its lessons from God, but is taking lessons about God.

Forty-two denials were found in the Egyptian Book of the Dead, to be said over. Five denials were first mentioned in Spiritual Science. Jesus, while dealing face to face, used seven.

After Jesus Christ threw off responsibility by assuming all the responsibility of the whole race and dissolving it, we were left with no denials.

III

AFFIRMATION

"And God saw the Light that it was good."
[Genesis 1:4]

"God is able of these stones to raise up children
unto Abraham." [Luke 3:8]

"And the third angel sounded and there fell a
great star from heaven, burning as it were a lamp,
and it fell upon the third part of the rivers, and
upon the fountains of waters; and the name of the
star is called wormwood." [Revelation 8:10]

The fact of Being is One—Undivided and Undividable One. Here is where we get our unit from, which has no origin in objects or imaginations. Where is the unit, one? We make a mark. That symbols it, but the mark is not the unit one. The undivided One is God—not man's imagination of a unit—not man's image of a great One on a throne—and into this One all things are resolved. It is not composed of particles, for then it could not be One. It would be many. So the One that is God is an inconceivably Small Point—too small to have particles—too small to be composed of anything.

How dazzling is the Point of Light which congeals or converges all the Light of the universe, far and near, into one Point, too small to have flames! For if the converged Point had flames, then it were not One!

How solid the substance that congeals all substances into its one Point! Too small to have particles, or atoms, or molecules, or points of gas, or cosmic dusts; for if the Point had so many places and ports, it could not be one undivided One. How lively the Life Point that converges all life into its one Point! How lovely the Love that congeals all love into its indivisible Self! This Point is God.

As the unit one seems to show multitudes of manufactures of itself, so God seems to be everywhere different. But it is all seeming, which makes Life seem differentiated. It is all seeming which makes Light seem different.

How marvelously the wisdom concentrates all wisdom into one Point! No wonder the Point sees Itself as Light all good. No wonder wisdom sees Itself as Wisdom all good. What is the difference between Light and Wisdom? No difference. Knowledge of Self is Light.

What is the difference between Light and Knowledge? No difference. If we make a candle flame, we are only making a mark to symbolize Knowledge, if we attempt to define Knowledge, we are where the boldest mathematician would be who should attempt to explain one. He can make a mark. We can make a flame.

But the Light is still the concentrated all in One. Jesus Christ said that God could take all the stones and make them children. They could be Abraham's children, all dropping from him. But Abraham should be faith, confidence, father, starting point, which should seem to be many points of departure but still is one point only.

We have the third angel's voice. It is the one Star—the doctrine of the shining Point. Man is composed of countless egos. An ego is an "I." One "I" says through him some way, "I am cold." Another "I" at the same moment says, "I am in pain." Another "I" at the same moment says, "I am hot."

These "I's" are marks. They are symbols like the mark "one" in mathematics. They are not the "I Point." They are the stones that are all to be made into live "I's" and merged into the Life Point. All the good of the universe is congealed into the Good Point. All the evil of the world is congealed into the evil point. If good/evil, light/wisdom are one indivisible One, then at the undifferentiated God-Point, evil and good cannot be separated.

The wormwood[6] to the rolling waters of the world is a symbol. Conscious minds object to having a Point in which evil and good are lost in the Undivided One.

There is no name for this Point except One. Our sacred books all point to a time when the "I" of all shall be Lord over all, so recognized by all. "In that day there shall be one Lord and his name One." [Zechariah 14:9]

The name of one set of egos all united in concentrated attention toward the Origin—the true "Ego"—was Jesus Christ. Another name of a set of egos all bent toward not seeming to be what they were not any more, was Buddha.

The Brahmins aver that with the proclamation to our set of egos or "I's," that they are no more in fact than marks of the unit, the end of mirages will be seen. The children, as stones, will be Abraham's life. Life and mind and faith will be merged in one Point; not newly merged, but no more marking—All Light, All Life, All Wisdom, One—no symbol.

---

[6] Wormwood is referred to in John's *Revelation* as a star that falls upon the earth when the third angel sounds and pollutes one-third of the world's rivers by making them bitter. The plant wormwood is a variety of *Artemesia* (named after the Syrian goddess, Artemis) and is used in the Old Testament as a metaphor for bitterness.

The book of Genesis was written by Esdras.[7] He was looking backward as a figure on the blackboard might look back to where it hailed from. There he suddenly saw what Moses taught. He saw it as symbol. This symbol is the first chapter of Genesis. It is a symbol because it tells of markings, movements, spreadings.

But even as a symbol it has the drawing power on our stony egos. They turn toward the one Point.

When each one sees itself turning back, its self seems to be its own starting point. They all feel the sharp refulgence of the concentrated Light Point, the star lesson. Their being drafted into one feeling is their sight of Good. It is their Light. It is their Life. It is their Love.

This accounts for men so often calling God, Good-Life-Truth-Love-Substance-Intelligence-Sight. It is their recognition, feeling, sight of the Starting Point. This is Light. How good it is! All the faculties alert to this, make the Jesus Christ man. Part of the faculties alert to this make a Joshua man, or Moses man, or Socrates man. No longer anything but the One Point—there you have "the

---

[7] Although tradition has it that Moses wrote the first five books of the Old Testament (called the *Pentateuch*), scholars agree that it was probably stories handed down from generation to generation, modified somewhat during the Babylonian captivity, and recorded by the first Scribes, notably a man named Esdras, about the time of the construction of Solomon's Temple in the last millennium before Christ.

Father and I are One." We are able to be all alert to One.

The study of this block of statements from the first page of this lesson to this paragraph will strike "One" in the being—will strike "One" on the chords of being.

Sharp Light Point into which all Light is concentrated is God. All the ideas of God held by all races of men must be melted into One. Their ideas of God are not God. They must see that their idea of God is nothing. This is wormwood to the waters or the conscious thoughts. They do not like to give up their thought idea of God. It is their proudest ego. They put their idea of God up high. But when we see that all ideas must be fused into an undividable One, there is no idea reigning over other ideas, prouder, nobler than they. There is no up-high one and down-low one. Here is the only One.

Thus, Mahomet/Mohammed, in the *Al-Koran*, tells us not to speak too low to the Deity and again not too loudly to the Deity. The last paragraph of his revelation called "Night Journey" shows that part of his egos were engaged in sighting the Light Point. Had all his faculties been engaged, he could not have told his men that they might rob a stranger, but a brother they might not rob. He could not have spoken of Moses as envious of him. This is the feeling of the Point being neither high to be shouted at nor low to be mumbled at:

> "Call upon God or call upon the Merciful; by whichso-
> ever of the two names ye invoke Him, it is equal; for He
> hath most excellent names. Pronounce not thy prayer
> aloud, neither pronounce it with too low a voice, but fol-
> low a middle way between these; and say, 'Praise be
> unto God, who hath not begotten any child; who hath no
> partner in the kingdom, nor hath any to protect him
> from contempt; and magnify him by proclaiming his
> greatness.[8]

This one paragraph epitomizes all the doctrines of all in One—all in the indivisible—all focused lights into One Light—all converged
substances into One Substance—the supreme
loss of the myriad markings and symbols into the
One Substance without symbol—all the stones to
be Abraham, which is faith, which is Father,
which is One Point, without Son, without offspring. John, the Revelator, speaks of there being
eventually no sea, that is, no seeming mind. All is
then the real Mind—The One.

Telepathy is symbol mind telling news to symbol mind. It may tell of the Divine One. Such a
message will destroy the human mind, leaving exposed the Divine Mind which does not communicate anything, as it has nobody to communicate
to. It is concentrated knowing already in Itself.
Mahomet/Mohammed sighted this with part of his
egos or human mind. In the measure that he
sighted it, he exposed Divinity. This gave his

---

[8] The *Koran.* Surah (refers to a chapter or section) XVII, [110-
111].

words strength. All the actions of human mind are actions of symbols, the same as figures on a blackboard. Back of the fleeting figures on the blackboard is the great fact. So back of the human mind which manufactures a river with one of its projecting thoughts and manufactures a brain with another of its projecting thoughts, stands the One Mind that manufactures nothing. It is already indivisible.

This is not a new doctrine, but is the unkillable philosophy of the Soul of man through countless ages. The instant the human mind looks this way for its thinking, we find the divine powers more nearly shadowed forth. To think of the Undividable One, will collect all the mental faculties into one concentrated Light. The mental faculties being focused, our bodily conditions speedily unite into a new comradeship.

Human mind being in the act of studying the One Point, becomes self-befriending. The troubles and vicissitudes of human life are owing to the unfriendliness of the subconscious thoughts and the conscious thoughts. The head is tired often, but the feet are refreshed. They should be utterly friendly. When friendly, all nature must point our affairs with prosperity in every way. As we stand at the foot of the stairway meaning to ascend, our feet do not ascend. They are shrewd. The mind accepts the refusal of the feet graciously. The stairs are on fire. The feet saw the hidden flames. Something in our human mind, some little ego, always tells which way to step. But no; the cross-grained ego that we have set up as king declares that the feet shall go up the stairs. So then all the egos must rouse themselves to protect life. There is no need to protect life. The only subject that should ever engross all the egos should be the Presence, Power and Science of the One. This is Life without protecting life; this is friendliness of all the faculties; then the wise feet are smiled upon by the wise ego that formerly was too proud to know the wisdom of the foot ego. The stones all become alive and friendly.

There is no science like the Science of the One.

"Seek ye first the kingdom of God and all these things shall be added unto you."

The covenant of the Lord is to perform without bestirring ourselves. Looking unto the one Lord, Lo! That is all we have to do.

Jesus had seen the One Point when He turned the water into wine. He had seen the One Point when He became a meek receptacle for all the sickness of Judea to fall into and He was not sick. He offered to be a receptacle for all the sin of the world, and be not Himself hurt by it. As you, by taking the hand of a palsied man, might take all his palsy into your system and then drop it into the ground at your feet, so Jesus stood in Galilee and still stands at your side—yea, even is now grounding you, and offers to take all your human mind with all its cares and terrors, and will as an Everlasting One drop them into the sands of oblivion. They shall be remembered no more against you forever.

"Acquaint now thyself with the Lord and be at peace."

1.Epicurus	Greek philosopher [342? -270 B.C.E.
2.Zeno	Greek philosopher of the 4th-3rd Century, B.C.E. Founder of the Stoic school.
3.Aristotle	Greek philosopher [384- 322 B.C.E]
4.Plato	Greek philosopher (427? -347 B.C.E.]
5.Pythagoras	Greek philosophers and mathematician. Died about 497 B.C.E
6.Agesilaus II	King of Sparta [400-360 B.C.E.].

What was Epicurus (1) the Greek, trying to do when he established a school to study the means of getting out of fear? He was feeling for the fearless One.

What was Zeno (2) trying to do when he founded a school in Athens to study Zeus, the primeval fire? He was seeking the Shining One.

What was Aristotle (3) trying to do when he announced his philosophy and gathered men to reason with him on the Primal Energy? He was calling all men to look backward toward their Starting Point.

What was Plato (4), Aristotle's teacher, struggling to do when calling men to look to the First Root of the universe, the God Spirit which propels all? He was feeling the drawing power of an ego in his realm of egos, as it caught a hint of the Invisible.

What was Pythagoras (5) trying to do in his school where the prime proposition was that the Soul is a self- moving Principle? Did he not catch a glimpse of the Independent One?

What was Jacob doing when wrestling with the invisible Spirit in the night-watches? Was he not rallying all his egos—all his faculties—to look straight to the One Presence in whom all things are finished? In whom all is Light? And in whose Light is that Good that has no opposite in evil?

When Agesilaus, (6) the aged King of Sparta, with a deformed body, a faltering tongue, could rally all his forces and defeat the young generals of other countries, what did his many egos practice? Simply sighting afar off the Invisible One!

Learn thou the Invisible One! By all attention, be the Invisible One. You came forth from the Invisible One. As a unit on the blackboard might eagerly seek for its origin, so turn to your Starting Point.

As Job reasoned with the Almighty till he caught sight enough to rise up conqueror; as the young Jesus talked to the Father till He held all His thoughts as one thought and managed waters, men, and death-so talk to your Starting Point.

Stop now and tell your Starting Point that you are ready to dissolve all your mind and body into It. Being dissolved in the Invincible One for one instant, you yourself shall arise invincible. Being aware that the objects in your room are only markings representing the Secret One, all Life, all Wisdom, all Good, you become aware of the One all Wisdom and you arise alt shining.

You are married to your One.

The first stone, or principal of God present among us, is Jasper, clear as crystal. This is the diamond. It is a marking symbol of the Word that cannot be broken. That Word is the Name, One.

The second stone is the sapphire—Purity, Aloofness. [That which is not One has no name.]

The third stone in Unity is the merging of all into One—identification with One—Union with One. It is chalcedony.

The call is to seek and see One; and all that the One is, we who see the One are sure to be.

IV

FAITH

"And God said. Let there be a firmament in the midst of the waters." [Genesis 1:6]

"And the fourth angel sounded and the third part of the sun was smitten, and the third part of the moon, and the third part of the stars, so as the third part of them was darkened, and the day shone not for the third part of it, and the night likewise. And I beheld, and heard an angel flying through the midst of heaven saying with a loud voice. Woe, woe, woe, to the inhabitants of the earth by reason of the other voices of the trumpets of the three angels which are yet to sound."
[Revelation 8:12-13]

The first lessons always deal with the divine ego whose throne is in the myself of each man.

The last six lessons always deal with the divine ego in the universe whose throne is everywhere equally present.

Moses and John clasp hands over the seas and sands of centuries in making the fourth lesson the doctrine of faith. Jesus had a doctrine of faith. All the inspired of the ages have had a doctrine of faith.

Faith is confidence. Faith is spiritual certainty without need of outward sight. Faith is substance. Faith is the body of the mind.

Paul thought that without faith it would be impossible to please God. By this he meant that the Divine Ego in the universe shows the divine power of man's Divine Ego when bold confidence on the part of the human ego rends the flimsy veil of hiding by being strictly certain that back of the human ego the Divine Fact abides; and through the universe the Divine Fact abides also. The human ego is glad to get out of the way. This is faith.

That which already is, is to be seen. Jesus insisted that the human ego, or lord of the body, ought to be very bold, violent, determined, firm, insistent. As: "The violent take the kingdom of God by force." These directions were in His fourth lesson. Every transaction pertaining to compelling things unseen to be seen, is a practice of firmness, that is, firm-a-ment or firm mind.

A man wished to call his friend from the world of the departed. Keeping very still, he firmly called mentally. He called again. He spoke the name as one determined to be heard. Soon an answer rang down the winds from without through the walls of his room: "I'm coming." He was too frightened to receive his mystic guest. It was night on this world's bosom, and the night terrifies the human ego.

This is only an illustration of the firmness with which the Divine Fact of the universe must be dealt with. While thus firm, the mind seems to change from its former substance, quavering and doubting, to a new Substance, steady and certain. But, if it is true that the Divine Ego in man is changeless, then is it not true that the human ego changes into the Divine? No. The human ego lets go being itself. It lets go being anything. By firmness, it rends itself apart and the Divine shines through.

The human mind is lord over all things by thousands, yea, even millions of methods. Its firmness is always needed in every method. No man succeeds on any lines without being firm in the right fashion. All firmness is hinting at that firmness Moses speaks of whereby the human rends itself like a veil and lets the Body—the Fact—the Substance that changes not, come into view. He was hinting at the same firmness that Jesus meant.

John means the firm angel by his talk of the fourth angel flying through the midst of heaven crying to the earth its woes because of what had been spoken by the first three angels and its woes to come by and other three angels yet to sound.

Earth is human ego. Its shape is like the earth. If you say, "The idea is on my mind that I am unhappy," you are speaking more nearly of the way the idea lives than if you say that it is in your mind. We are in the human "I am" as earth. The three lessons in Judgment do sound woe to the human ego, because they prefer it to rend itself. The other three angels are a woe to the human ego indeed if the first three have been heard, for the human ego cannot then be found. The only Presence then is the Divine; the woes are fulfilled. The rending of the human mind is its departure. Its rending is its own doing. Its rending is sure if it has heard the messages of the first three lessons aright.

The human mind gets conscious of there being a Spiritual manner of hearing. Then the human mind begins to throw off its ideas from its surface as one might swing his arms and throw aside things hovering in the air.

The sun of mind is intellect till the Spiritual Sun is heard about. Then the interest the human ego takes in being intellectual wanes. He does not care any more for his intellect. John said this was the sure effect of hearing the first three lessons in Judgment [Revelation 8:12].

The human ego is as a weather vane, turning first to one wind that blows and then to another, all the time in hope of finding something to believe in sufficiently to disappear. Notice how your mind is always searching for that in which you may repose absolute confidence. You rest it in a religion, but then suddenly find that you are as unsatisfied as ever. The religion has not preserved you from calamity, nor brushed aside your pain. You repose for awhile in a friend, but suddenly the friend is gone. You realize the instability of all things. It is the weather vane trick of mind or the human ego. Find the Stable One.

"Let the Lord be thy confidence; He will not suffer thy feet to be taken." There is One God who is above you all and through you all and in you all. This God changes not. The Kingdom of God changes not. Eye hath not seen it. Mind hath not imagined it. But confidence in the super-incumbence of an eternal and changeless Presence makes an entirely new outlook in your life. Your eyes see better conditions. Your mind feels happier.

The new conditions are not the visibility of the true Kingdom. The happy mind is not heaven. The confidence of the mind that rends itself to the extent that Jesus Christ taught must be spoken of by us and realized by all who know about that Jesus Christ mind in themselves, as utterly indifferent to environments. The highest state of faith is beyond environments.

If the Divine Ego were glad because I were happy. and mournful because I were mourning, then it were as undesirable to be Divine as human. "God seeth not as man seeth."

"Infinity is bliss," said Gautama, the Buddha. This is why looking towards the Changeless One brings happy changes. We look by a firm mind. With our eyes of mind fixed always towards the Changeless One, we rally a mysterious confidence. We know that no evil can touch us. There is one promise of the Divine and Changeless that is strength even to read it over: "I will contend with him that contendeth against thee." Confidence, which is faith, soon rises so strong that no amount of cumulated disadvantages dismays you. The One in whom confidence is put is equal to quelling the stormiest seas. The highest mountains of difficulty fade into misty nowhere.

"The Eternal God is thy refuge, and underneath are the Everlasting Arms." The Jesus Christ Mind in every man is the Jesus Christ Mind that charges the universe with safety. "Look unto me and be ye saved."

The safety of a man is his faith. "If a man have confidence," says the Shinto religious teacher, "though he place that confidence in a sardine's head, it will do what he expects." Confidence is in itself a render of films.

Look at Elisha hulling out bread enough from the ten loaves to feed a hundred young men. Look at him rending the film from a handful of salt and disclosing its healing properties. Others might practice putting salt into water but only to make it taste worse than ever. Elisha had such confidence that the healing power of the spirit of the universe was bound to be disclosed, even through the grains of salt.

The healing power in this universe was once given the name "Jesus Christ." Is not that as good a name as "God?" Suppose the adepts of the Orient can charge a name with such energy that whenever it is spoken, a miracle is wrought. They have in times past so charged certain names. This is the case with the Name "Jesus Christ." One came who so filled His own Name with His omnipotent faith, that it is His own healing power, prospering power, wisdom power, to this day. He called the omnipotent Spark that shines in all men, by His own Name.

He called the omnipotent Fire that shines back of and through all things by His own Name.

Whatever great work you would see performed, call the Power by which it is to be worked out by the name He gave directions to call it, and see if it will not demonstrate in your having a strong confidence first, and then seeing the mighty deed wrought out afterward. "Whatsoever ye shall ask the Father in My Name, He will give you."

Take that text for a fact. Take that Spark of Divinity that shines in you and call it the Jesus Christ in you. Tell it what you want done. Tell it what you want the God in the universe to perform for you.

Call it by its rightful Name. Call again. Call firmly. You are speaking to the Omnipotent Spark in your being. It will force you to feel confidence as a magnet forces a steel needle to be magnetic. And your confidence may be so absolute that you are no longer among us as human, but are present all Divine. You have faith in God. You have the faith of God. You are God.

The waters of changing thoughts come and go. One day it is gloom, the other it is gladness. The lesson of Moses was: "Let there be a firmament in the midst of the waters."

You have the power to be firm. God is, and God is present. Be firm. Call on God. Call again. Be determined not to be refused. The God in you has supreme rights in the universe. The God in the universe can be plainly seen by insisting.

It is true that human affairs move and stir and change. "But I am the Lord, I change not." It does not make human affairs or human mind real to say they change. There is no reality in them. The reality that fills the very place that they seem to occupy is the changeless God. It does not make the human mind a reality to describe its glooms and pleasures. The reality that occupies the very place where the human mind seems to be is the Divine Mind.

When one calls a chair "God" he means that his confidence in God is so strong that he feels God there where it looks like a chair. There is no chair there. God only is there. Where the human mind claims to be, God only is there. The chair and the mind that formulates chairs are both absent.

God is here. The unreal is nothing. The real is all. The real is alive, intelligent, reliable. It never loses intelligence, life, reliability. We are capable of seeing the real by rending the veil and flying between the two parts thereof as John saw the angel flying. An angel is a firm, beautiful message. It is a dart of Truth that cuts the mental cataracts open. The hopes of heaven and the beliefs of earth are rolled aside.

The heaven that the human mind has longed for is described as a state opposite to Hades. But God, the true kingdom, is not opposite to anything. It is noticed, Paul said, that we never rend the veil in this age by the word of God. We rend it by the word Jesus Christ. The lesson cuts the cataract over your mind's attention is the lesson on faith that shows your human mind how to stop describing heaven and earth, and see the real heaven and the real earth that the Jesus Christ spark in you, your real self, sees. If we describe our unfortunate affairs, we see them. If we describe a heaven and a hell, we shall see them.

A mystic traveled in a trance to a place where he saw millions of people in fiery torments. He had an angel with him who told him these people had described hell all their human days and were now realizing it. Did that make the hell real? By no means. It only showed the mystic the eventual power of insistence. He spoke to them loudly to call their attention. "These fires are not real!" he shouted. "You manufacture bogus conditions by firmly believing in them. Start up yourselves and declare firmly that they are nothing—nothing—nothing. Declare firmly the Name, Jesus Christ. That is the name of that principle within you that does not see these fires and never agreed with your mind when it was believing in fires! The everlasting God puts no one in hell. You may dissolve your own manufactures."

Such sublime looks as these self-condemned creatures gave!

Paul speaks of preaching to the spirits in prison. He doubtless had seen the multitudes of people who had talked firmly of punishments of God till they were shut into walls of imagination. Ezekiel speaks of those in the walls of imagery. Thus the human mind is found incapable of describing either heaven or hell.

Are you satisfied with the heaven St. John pictures? Are you satisfied with the heaven the Spiritualists describe? Are you satisfied with the heavens Swedenborg tells of? Are you satisfied with Mahomet's description of heaven? But there is something in you that can describe heaven and earth exactly. You believe in this something within you. There is Something present everywhere that knows the exact description.

This message of Science is the angel that cuts the mind. It is the doctrine of confidence. If you do not like to place your confidence in that inward one that is the real Myself of you by calling it Jesus Christ pray tell what is its better name? If you have the confidence to tell it you cannot name it, but would like to see it take all your life in hand, you can do so. You have one message only on this point and that is, "Be firm!" Hold your own while the waters of your daily lot sweep by you. David said, "The proud waters have rushed over me, but in Thee do I trust."

Jesus called this Father. He looked toward Himself. He saw it abode in Himself. He had confidence in the mightiness of His Myself. He looked up toward heaven and there also He saw the Father. He had confidence in the mightiness of the Myself that fills the universe.

He utterly rent Himself as human, and the Father, the Divine, the God of Him, stood forth. He saw. He sees. He knows the real heaven and the real earth. This He told over and over. He charged Himself with His own divinity by ceasing to be human. He had wrapped the veil of the human around Himself like the rest of us. He took on the human and then made that human dissolve itself by confidence in the Divine. Thus, His Name stands as the rending of the veil of the temple. The Holy of Holies is the Divine in Myself. The Holy of Holies is the Divine in the universe. If the human veil hides the Holy One, the human veil must be rent.

This is done by firm confidence, firm insistence. The judgment day of mind is come when all the lessons or angels are sounded. The judgment of mind is gone by, and it needs no longer any judgment when all human heavens and hells are gone. Why conjure up any world to fasten yourself into by imagining firmly, steadily till it comes, if the Jesus Christ in you is in the true, the real, the unimagined kingdom? Did not John say at the last, after he had described his idea of heaven, that it had not entered into the heart of man to conceive the real heaven and the real earth, but that Jesus Christ knew all about it? That Jesus Christ he spoke of is the God in you.

"Whosoever confesseth that Jesus Christ is God hath life."

Whatever be your name for the Mighty One within you, be sure you pursue it firmly. Whatever be your name for the Mighty One filling the universe, be sure you call it firmly.

If you call angels, angels will arrive. If you call devils, devils will come. Such a power lies in firmness to bring to pass. If you call Jesus Christ, Jesus Christ will come—as heaven, as earth, as light, as joy, as home, as the Everlasting God.

V

WORKS

*"And God said, let the waters be gathered together
in one place and let the dry land appear."
[Genesis 1:9]*

*"And the fifth angel sounded, and I saw a star fall
from heaven unto the earth, and to him was given
the key of the bottomless pit." [Revelation 9:1]*

In all Spiritual Science there are twelve proc-
lamations which constitute the Tree of Life. This,
then, is really what is meant by the Tree of Life,
namely, Spiritual Science. This Tree of Life bears
twelve manners of fruits. [Revelation 22:2]

In pure Science there need be but one word. If
that word is spoken, the twelve fruits will be visible. That one word is the lost word, so-called, because no one can, by speaking any one word that

he knows, cause all the twelve fruits to fall upon his earth.

The first lesson in Spiritual Science is called The Word. The second lesson is called Denial. The third lesson is called Affirmation. The fourth lesson is called Faith. The fifth lesson is called Works. The sixth lesson is called Understanding. The seventh is called Inheritance. The eighth is called Truth. The ninth is called Holiness. The tenth is called Forgiveness. The eleventh is called Wisdom. The twelfth is called Free Grace.

These names of the twelve lessons are modified somewhat, or changed enough to put in different terms through the metaphysical books of every age. They may all be summed up in one word. This word is the Tree of Life to him that can pick it out of the combined twelve.

There are twelve fruits from this Tree of Science. We are always telling over the twelve signs of the Spirit in man. There is one fruit we call life; another we call health; another, strength; another, prosperity; another, protection; another is mind; another, speech; another is writing; another is singing; another is judgment; another is praise.

The lost word was once known to man, we are told. It was whispered in the ear of each new keeper of it and by him was held sacred. There is a tradition that the compiler of the Sohar[9] was the last man who held this word. He is reported to

---

[9] In other places, she spells this guide to the Kabbala, Zohar.

have been in constant danger of death from enemies, and had to live in a guarded cave. As one of
the twelve fruits of the Tree of Life is absolute
safety, we *are* able to detect at once that he did
not have the lost word which in itself is the whole
Tree of Life or whole Science of God.

If, under the dispensation of these twelve lessons (which can by any one who has received the
fruit of good judgment, be put into one lesson)
there is any disease left in our teacher of them, he
certainly has not tasted of the Tree of Life; he does
not know Spiritual Science.

If he is afraid of anyone or of anything, he has
not found Spiritual Science. He may be seeking it,
and he may appreciate that the whole Science is
wrapped up in his own Spirit, but he is not yet the
Tree of Life in himself letting fall twelve manner of
fruits, one fruit of which is safety. "A thousand
may fall at thy right hand, and ten thousand at
thy left hand, but it shall not come nigh thee." "He
shall deliver thee in six troubles, yea, in seven
there shall no evil touch thee."

Now, if one tells us that persecution, rage,
hunger, trouble, are the sure lot of the Christian,
we may take the names of the fruits known to
grow on the Christian Tree and not one wilt ever
be found under any of these heads. It will be
safety. Jesus, the Christian, said, "If a man keep
my sayings, he shall never see death."

Moses was said to be in possession of the lost
word. By it he wrought miracles. He was not

afraid of kings and armies, and he never died. In his fifth lesson he repeats the first lesson under another figure. The Tree of Life, or the Science of the Name that is not spoken, is called waters and land. As the waters form the land, so Science adjusts a man's whole life.

"Behold I set all things in order when I come"

Beware, then, for though a man may be brilliant and powerful in speech, he must have a wonderful and miraculous life or he is not talking strict Science.

By this restatement of the first lesson, Moses means that this man who is talking partly the Science of God and partly his human concept, will have a life just like his talk. It will be mixed. The land will show how his flowing thoughts that speak so handsomely and then so badly, are working. "Let this law of mind be plain," said Moses, through Esdras, namely, that your lot will keep tally with your mind. If your mind is rent apart for the God mind to be all there is of you, then your wonderful life conditions will show the same to your whole universe. If you are still firmly abiding by human insistences, your environments will tally with that kind of mind.

If a man wants to reap what he has not sown, he must be rent asunder and lost to the human, that the firm unspeakable splendor of the Divine may be manifest.

Surely a man did not sow the kingdom of the eternal, and reap a harvest of the eternal! He only manages human affairs by the water-like force of mind. He rends his human mind and he sees the water and land of God.

"Let a man see these," said Moses. Let him see the everlasting kingdom.

The text of this lesson touches your case if you are dwelling on the intellectual plane where you are continually taking notice of what thoughts you formed your conditions out of, or whether you are watching the Divine Presence and know that your thoughts are of no account to it whatsoever.

If you see a ragged woman picking up faggots,[10] you may know she is one of your thoughts pushed into your sight. One of your thoughts is a shabby, unhappy, begging thought. It may be about one subject and it may be about another. Perhaps you think God has left you out of a home while He has given others good homes. That thought keeps tagging you up, and exhibiting itself before you in the tattered, unhappy form of some poor person all the time. Change that thought. Take a new premise. Look at your mighty Soul. Is it homeless? Looking at that Soul and calling it by the true Name will sweep every beggar off your earth. The beggars are not real, they are pictures of your thoughts.

The only poor that Jesus spoke of was the poverty of the living God; the poor in spirit. God is

---

[10] The word "faggots" refers to pieces of firewood cut to fit a small woodstove—usually about 3" thick and 15" long.

not spirit. He owns no spirit. God is not matter. He owns no matter. The absolutely Poor is God-pure nothing.

The word, "nothing," is a name of the indwelling One which is your Myself. It is one name of the One that inhabits eternity-the universe. This Poor, or Nothing, is what Jesus said He should be. "The poor ye have always with you." "Lo! I am always with you."

When he said, "Me ye have not always with you," He meant that form of a man He then had. He should remove that out of their sight according to their request. "Depart out of our coasts," they had requested. "Depart off this planet," was their command. He always answers every prayer. The firm insistence of any crowd of people upon either the absence of a perfect man or the presence of all perfect men, is sure to be obeyed. This takes us to the fifth angel, Works: key to the bottomless pit; Star that fell from heaven to earth.

The bottomless Pit is the "I AM" in man. Into it all death, all hell, all heavens, all earth, are to fall. "He will swallow up death." [Isaiah 25:8] Who is this that is able to swallow up death? Only the One that is All. Only One is able to hold all things and able to hold more after they are swallowed. That is the "I AM."

John sees misery departing into the mouth of the "I AM" exactly as Moses saw his fears, his weaknesses, his stammering, his human nature, departing into the awful Splendor and Majesty of the "I AM." If we were to take Moses alone for our authority on naming that mystic region of our being which is not mixed up with any of our human lot and speech, we should call it the "I AM." If we take the four gospels and John, the Revelator, we should know that its old Name was "I AM," but its new Name is Jesus Christ. If we believe the New Testament, we shall believe that the Name Jesus Christ is the key to the lost word, for we are told that in that Name is a New Name.

Thus the lesson on Works is a name which unlocks the bottomless pit or opens the "I AM"-opens the door that shows the Unnamable One. It gives us the lost word with which all the universe is manageable without our effort.

The compiler of the Sohar was named Ben-lochai. He said he held the mercaba, or the power to open a mind's eyes to see into the "I AM." That is, he was speaking exactly what John means by the Star that held the Key. Ben-lochai said he held the Key to Sight.

We are to see the kingdom of the "I AM"—the "Bottomless Pit"—the "Absolutely Poor"—the "Swallower of all things."

The bird flying south sees the realm of splendor by firm confidence. When she gets there she sees it face to face. Thus, Moses speaks of seeing the realm of God, which was not made by any kind of thought to one, and to another, he speaks of seeing whatever kind of land, or home, or friend, or power, has been firmly thought about.

Be not confused.

The lesson on Works shows that you make your environment as much by what you do not think as by what you do think.

You do not think how the kingdom of God looks. You know it is within you. So you look towards it and call it by Name, either what Moses told you or what Jesus told you. The Name means nothing to you? Very well, you are surely not thinking anything while you are looking toward the Swallower within you.

What was one of Jesus Christ's fifth lessons? This: "In such an hour as ye think not, the Son of Man cometh." His "Son of Man" meant the Divinity within you that sets your life in order for you. Moses knew this. He also knew that for the lightest word we give account. Our lot in life distinctly pictures our secret words, our audible words, our written words. Words are waters. All solid appearances are land.

The Brahmins teach that the Absolute and Eternal God was originally one Point, but diffused Himself abroad. Thus all the spreading worlds beyond worlds and ethers beyond ethers are the extension of the God Point which was once infinitesimally small.

The spreading abroad is the day of Brahman. The drawing together again is the night of Brahman. They teach that we are now all tending to unity, and this shows that Brahman is drawing

Himself together. By their teaching we are hastening into the night.

What a variety of explanations man has made to account for Brahman or God! Why does man imagine such fantastic notions and by holding them firmly, finally see them? Is it a necessity of his mind that he formulate and formulate and formulate, first one globe to dwell upon, then another? Is not his life well with him when he finds God?

Jesus Christ, speaking of your money matters, your health, your protection, and how to work them into good states, said: "Seek ye first the Kingdom of God and all these things shall be added unto you." His doctrine of works was so entirely different from other men's doctrines that it has not even yet been thought practical. Take no thought—no thought at all—about what ye shall eat. Who even in the high reasonings of Spiritual Science has told you that you need not say mentally that you should be fed well? Have we not been carefully taught to mentally proclaim that we are always well fed? But Jesus said: "Do not think about it at all." God will feed you anyway. Seek his kingdom; that is the main thing,

How shall we seek if we do not think anything? He replies: "Look!" We do have a looking power that is not with our eyesight. We can do this looking while we have our eyes shut. We are able to see face to face, our Divinity Point that is our God indwelling.

The firm naming of his friend by the young man mentioned in the fourth judgment lesson was swiftly bringing the friend from the realm of the invisible into plain sight. He would not be calling that name over and over when he got him near him, but would talk about other things or be silent. Thus, the firm naming of the Divine Presence by the Name "Jesus Christ" soon brings something so close that we cannot speak. This is the unspeakable Gift. Paul said he found what it was not lawful to utter. So his life was a blaze of miracles. Every life is a blaze of miracles when it is set to moving by either the Name of our Divine Nature or by getting beyond the ability to call the Name, being lifted into unspeakable states.

If you will notice, while you are speaking to the Divine in your sick neighbor, you forget to speak. This is the miracle-working moment. There is a line of reasoning on the mere subject of healing. The reasoning is very absorbing. "Let us have a reason for the hope that is in us," said Peter [1Peter 3:15). Reasoning is water. The sudden stopping of reasoning is the sure sign that the work is done.

Read the book *Natural Law in the Spiritual World* (by Henry Drummond) for a good reasoning on healing. But know this, that in all cases it is at some point where you are too entranced to reason that the healing is done.

So with your own Divine Nature. You call it the "I AM," or you call it "Jesus Christ," or you describe it by some such name as "Bottomless Pit" or "Absolutely Poor" or "Swallowing One"—there comes a moment when you cannot call its Name. This moment is your life made over by a miraculous change. You step into the "Abysmal Dark" or into your own indwelling kingdom. This is works.

Books are certain kinds of reasonings. They are the strong water-flow that builds affairs. The Bibles of the world are responsible for the world's affairs. If they have not been clear, beautiful, unadulterated reasoning, how could they accomplish anything?

When pure and undefiled water is set flowing, it melts rocks. When pure reasoning is set flowing, all evil must dissolve. John, the Revelator, saw a picture of the earth dissolving because a pure doctrine had come.

This is pure doctrine, this Spiritual Science, which strikes at your judgment center and says:

What do you call the Supreme thing?

Where is the Supreme one?

What happens if you see the Supreme face to face?

This is pure doctrine, which explains that your reasoning well makes your life—If you reason that all is well because God is Supreme Good, your life will show it.

If you are firm in declaring what you have heard, you will see face to face. If you see face to face, you do not speak. Then a miracle is wrought.

The reading over of your *Judgment Series* lessons will give you a line of reasoning concerning your own Divine Ego. They will call Its name by the New Testament Name. You will be firm in the word till it puts you into the unspeakable. This may take you a year or it may take you three moments. There is no reckoning of time in Jesus Christ or in Spiritual Science.

The whole principle is, speak till your looking power is called into prominence. Keep on speaking till you cannot speak. Then you see, hear, touch, the miracle-working Presence. Not intensely, not laboriously, not as one who fights air, but as one who knows he is to see wonderful things come to pass soon, so shall you reason with your indwelling Almighty One as Job reasoned. See the miraculous efficiency of Job's reasoning. See the miraculous efficiency of Job's firm insistence.

Let your mind be firm until you have no mind. Then you see face to face.

The motto of this fifth lesson might be: "The less effort I make, the more I accomplish; and the nearer nothing I am, the greater my efficiency." For, as Elisha's bones raised a man to life, being trained down to nothingness by confidence, the sight, hearing, touch, smell, taste, of the new country are ours.

Martin Luther ceased from praying because though many miles distant from the scene of his persecutors, he saw and heard them grant him free speech on Protestantism.

So a mother ceased praying for her child's life. She saw the happy child run towards her. The prayer of faith stops your praying at all for a blessing because the blessing is plainly in sight. The confidence in your Divine Ego and its mighty kindness stops your naming it. You see what you had never expected to see, you hear new songs. Life begins over again.

What a man sees when he has spoken the Divine Name till it bursts its land and water on his sight, he hath never yet put into words. He walks on highways of delight. His kingdom has come.

VI

UNDERSTANDING

"And God saw that it was good." [Genesis 1:10]

"And the sixth angel sounded, and I heard a voice from the four horns of the golden altar which is before God, saying to the sixth angel which had the trumpet. Loose the four angels which are bound in the great river Euphrates." [Revelation 9:13-14]

"And it shall come to pass in that day, I will hear, saith the Lord. I will hear the heavens, and they shall hear the earth." [Hosea 2:21]

"O Lord, I beseech thee, send now prosperity. Blessed be he that cometh in the Name of the Lord. We have blessed you out of the house of the Lord." [Psalms 118:25-26]

That which we really see, we understand. Does God really see, or see unreally? It is written as supernal Truth that God sees that all is good. Does God really hear, or hear unreally? It is written as supernal Truth that whoever cometh in the right Name, the only God there is does certainly hear him.

In the right Name must certainly mean in the right Spirit. A child who wanted help repeated the alphabet over to the Lord God believing that she must give the most precious knowledge she possessed unto that Presence, and the alphabet was the only thing she had ever learned except the names of common objects. Her prayer was answered almost instantaneously by a miracle.

"Blessed be he that cometh in the Name of the Lord; we have blessed you out of the house of the Lord." (the Psalms of David) Then all the adversity of a people is because that people came not up to the house of the Lord of bounty in the right Spirit. David approached in the right Spirit and asked for prosperity. "O Lord, I beseech Thee, send now prosperity." [Psalms 118:25] He was answered immediately.

The sixth angel of judgment is the angel that teaches the Spirit of prosperity without delay.

Every lesson in Spiritual Science is but a repetition of the first lesson. Let this be understood. Moses suggested twelve repetitions. Jesus chose twelve disciples, each representing a lesson. John, the Revelator, chose twelve stones, each standing for a lesson well received. He also spoke of seven lessons; these might be called six days' messages and the Sabbath message. The six angels of the morning were always accompanied by a voice which spoke to the universe.

Everything runs from the character of the ego to its world. Whatever we are in our language, our world will present to our eyes. Simon Peter could rouse the power of the whole twelve lessons into one. He converted 3,000 by one sermon. His hearers were roused to heal the sick, feed the hungry, raise the dead, comfort the heart.

The sixth lesson represents the Divine Ego as understanding itself, and as itself is all there is to understand, it therefore understands all that is. The Divine Ego is God, and God sees all as good. The Divine Ego has its abode in you who read this page. It spreads itself everywhere and thus meets itself everywhere. The human ego also meets itself everywhere in exact imitation of the Divine. The human is the shadow of the Divine, taking up no room whatsoever in the realm of God, as shadows never take up any room anywhere.

Berkeley and Schopenhauer found out that there was no hot or cold, only as they formulated them. If a thing was hot to them, it was hot. If an orange was sweet to them, it was sweet. To others, the heat and the sweetness were not as to them. Thus they found that things and objects had no properties only as they gave them to them. And they also found that when pushed to the real facts of the case, things themselves did not exist, except as they formulated them. At first this is not apparent. You do not see it—that is, you do not understand it. You do not hear it-that is, your mind does not catch its verity—that is, again, you do not understand it.

But finally you do see. You understand. Now push your understanding hard enough to realize that there is something about you that sees everything good. There is nothing but its own kind, the creations of its understanding to it everywhere it goes. To that one in you there is no evil. Itself being Divine, all it sees is Divine. It understands itself. It understands that it meets itself everywhere it turns.

When the human mind sees that it meets itself everywhere it turns, meets things and people exactly like itself whether it likes them or not, then the human mind sees the advisability of getting an understanding of itself. The human mind discovers that if it can only understand itself, it will soon fix up the world to suit itself. It will decline to have any more miserable existences crawling around and fighting on this globe under an atmospheric sea about 40 miles deep, like a set of unhappy crustaceans.

So the high philosophy of Greece had the motto: "Know thyself." They had an understanding in the philosophic halls that the oracles would answer each idea. That makes it attraction. Let that idea be upturned or let it expect its fulfillment from above.

"Every good and perfect gift cometh from above." That is aspiration. Let it be upturned, or upcast long enough to ascend into the place where nothing can interfere with it to pull it down into another kind of quality. This is ascending; the child wished for some event to transpire and brought it down with her alphabet. David wished for prosperity to his throne, and brought it down with his: "Lord, help."

These characteristics were all employed by one who found that His Divine Ego was His only reality. The throwing aside of the whole realm of humanity that the splendid light of Divine understanding might shine out; the Divine can be seen when each of us is seen. This was John's meaning. He was not thinking of prosperity on any other plane than the manifestation of the Divine Man everywhere. Neither was Moses. But David and the child were both thinking of prosperity on the human plane brought there by calling upon the Divine. On this subject, Jesus would say, "If you seek the Divine Ego alone, try to know nothing else, be innocent of all else—you will find that your throne will be prospered, if you are a king, and you will find yourself satisfied with what new life happens unto you, if you are a peasant."

We are already in the realm of the Divine. It is the privilege of our senses to appreciate it. The Divine Ego looking toward our human, sees no human. It sees Itself. It sees the Divine. Jesus, looking around upon the people, said: "Who are my mother and my brethren? They that do the will of God." He saw His own kith and kin everywhere. They were not human beings to Him. He was teaching the omnipresence of the Divine and He saw and felt it everywhere.

He who has by firm insistence begun to see the Divine in himself, finds himself understanding the Divine. What he understands, he finds no fault in. (The presence of something to find fault about, is evidence of not understanding.)

Prosperity that comes from sighting and touching the Divine Ego is that understanding which makes you able to touch the right springs and get satisfaction out of everything in every direction.

Friends are not better to give you their jets of shining joy. Father, husband, brother, son, pauper, prince, one and all exposed one Nature. You understand that Nature. You deal with It alone. You are innocent of any other. Therefore, you draw it by like attracting like. You are looking to the highest, which is all that is real; thus you ascend into heaven. This is prosperity. All Bibles teach that prosperity is being all one with the Divine and seeing all Divine

The cases of answers to prayer are illustrative on simple planes of the answering Power of God without to the God within. "It shall come to pass in that day, that I will hear the heavens and they shall hear the earth." [Hosea 2:21]

Responsiveness is understanding. "They that understand among the people shall be wise and do exploits."

If you are on the plane of matter, you investigate matter. You study insects, or stones, or electricity. Finally they respond to you. They tell you their ways. Then you are reported to understand them. You are wise in them. You instruct the people therein. So on the purely Divine plane. You watch for the God in yourself as a man watches for the morning. You feel the Divine breaking through you. "This is my body broken for you," or breaking through you. Then you look up with your whole being alert. The God in the universe responds to you. Now you understand God. Everywhere you turn, all things work together for your prosperity. You know nothing but prosperity.

This is the way the sixth lesson in Spiritual doctrine always turns. It handles it in the first lesson under the head of understanding. It speaks of God as understanding. "I am understanding. I have strength." [Proverbs 8:14]

Nobody is so strong as he who has understanding of his subject. Von Moltke would sit silently by, while the Generals were discussing the army movements. He understood what they were all driving at. He saw their goal. He saw their methods. He knew what they wanted. He saw it. This made him wise in methods. With one sentence, he would outline a whole campaign. With his eye on victory, the way was clear. So with man's eye on God, his way is clear. He understands God, therefore his path is plain.

"The steps of the God man are ordered of the Lord."

There is no doubt about a certain kind of understanding of mathematics coming to one who studies numbers and nothing else. But now, suppose that by understanding God, the whole of mathematics might be revealed to you in one stroke? There is no prosperity in mathematics equal to that, is there?

There is surely a kind of understanding of languages certain to one who studies languages faithfully. But now, suppose that by understanding the Divine Presence, all languages should be yours in the twinkling of an eye? Is not this prosperity in language?

There is no doubt about a man's being able to get gold, who attends to nothing else but money. But now, suppose all the riches he could name should be his in one instant, by understanding God? That would be prosperity from above.

"Therefore, with all thy getting, get understanding," said Solomon.

Get understanding of God. For in God are all things. God is the source of all. The "four golden horns around His altar" are the four strong, everlasting calls to man not to be attentive to the animal, vegetable, mineral, intellectual kingdoms. Loose the angelic powers within you. Let them lay hold on God alone.

While artlessness, attractiveness, aspiration and ascension are hidden, you show their human shadows: approbativeness, amativeness, ambition, acquisitiveness. The four beautiful angels are covered with these four veils. So by their advice, man studies the animal plane, the vegetable plane, the mineral plane. The end is death.

"There is a way that seemeth right unto a man, but the end thereof are the ways of death." [Proverbs 14:121]

The end of the understanding of God is life. "This is eternal life, that ye know God." "In the way of righteousness is life, and in the pathway thereof there is no death."

The name of the understanding that you had with the Father before the world was, is your own Name. Your understanding is your own Name. No man knows his own Name, save he that has arrived at his own understanding.

If you know your understanding of stones, you may know that you have that name among all the people. What you understand of insects is your reputation. So what you understand of God is your reputation. It cannot be hidden. "No man lighteth a candle and putteth it under a bushel." You cannot hide the light of your understanding. The altar fire of your life is your understanding of God.

Look at the crowds you meet upon the streets. They all understand something of God. If they understand much, their eyes shine with steady light. There is a nameless prosperity about them. Surrounded by the four walls of the human mind, they yet do open windows now and then for the fire of their first and native understanding of God to shine through. They make rifts in the outward seeming for the inward light to stream through.

Shall not all your understanding stream forth when you have loosed the four angels ? Shall not the understanding of the animal kingdom stream forth from your central understanding of God? Shall not the full understanding of the vegetable kingdom stream forth brightly when your native understanding of God breaks forth? Shall not all the minerals of the universe be bright to your knowledge by the setting free, to stream over them, your knowledge of God? Shall not the intellectual kingdom be understood by you when your native understanding breaks forth?

Shall not that in them which has been a sealed book to the scholars of the world be clearly known to you when you throw the beams of your own understanding over them? The name, understanding, is one of your own names. What do you understand of yourself?

Moses saw that everything was good to God. Is not your God at your point of understanding? Is not one name of God, Understanding? Is not the tongue of inspiration the pen of the inspired, that always says of Jehovah, the Shining One, "I am Understanding"?

I understand. I am Understanding. I understand the secrets of the universe where I walk. I see God everywhere. I understand God.

Is not God's sight the real sight? Yet He beholds not iniquity. "There is no iniquity with the Lord our God, and no respect of persons." [II Chronicles 19:7]

Jesus Christ is another name for pure understanding. The name of your own understanding is Light. The Light of the world is its understanding. All the understanding of mankind that is visible is focused in one picture on the skies, called the sun. There is no physical sun in the skies. There is a picture of the combined understanding of the race of men as it has broken through the human mind. When the human mind is no longer a name to itself, being turned into entire openness, being self—rent all the Light of man is liberated.

"The city had no need of the sun, for the Lamb was the Light thereof."

The adepts of the Orient can liberate the astral light with which our atmosphere is flooded. The understanding of the "I AM"—the indwelling Light—the Jesus Christ—with which man is flooded—charged full- will liberate the everlasting One—the Lamb—the Light of the World. How lamblike and silent rests your own understanding within you! How lamblike and silent rests the understanding in the universe! The disappearance of the last trace of darkness is the shining of your understanding. To it, all is good. It sees itself. The hand of the Divine everywhere meets your touch. Heaven is happy greeting, responsiveness, understanding.

Take Saturday morning to proclaim understanding, to call the Jesus Christ in you, the Understanding One.

The twelve stones of the new city are the names of the One within you. The sixth is Sardius, the Shining One, the Light.

In the morning, sow your seed, and in the evening, withhold not your hand, for you know not what a day may bring forth, you know not which it shall bring forth, whether this or that.

Seeds are names of the One that abides in you.

The first lesson is the Name: The Word—"The Word was God."

The second lesson is your Name: your free, unburdened Soul, "What shall it profit a man if he gain the whole world and lose his own soul?"— that is, lose sight of his free spirit.

The third is your Name: Your affirmative One— that in you which says, "I AM."

The fourth is your Name: Your firm, changeless One.

The fifth is your Name: Your working One, your conquering One, "Yea, before the day was, I am He! And there is none that can deliver out of my hand. I will work and none can hinder."

The sixth is your Name: Your understanding One—with understanding, there is no fault, no mistake—there is no sight of flaws.

The Jesus Christ in you throws His Light on the world; and in that Light, all is heaven.

VII

INHERITANCE

*"And God said. Let the earth bring forth grass,
the herb yielding seed, and the fruit tree yielding
fruit, after its kind, whose seed is in itself."
[Genesis 1:1 1]*

*"And the seventh angel sounded; and there were
great voices in heaven, saying. The kingdoms of
this world are become the kingdoms of our Lord,
and of His Christ; and He shall reign forever and
forever. And the four and twenty elders, which sat
before God on their seats, fell upon their faces."
[Revelation 1 1:15-16]*

*"Bring forth, therefore, fruits meet for repentance."
[Matthew 3:8]*

The seventh lesson is always Inheritance. Inheritance is offspring. Offspring is fruits.

The first lesson of John, the forerunner of Jesus, was Repentance. The first lesson of Jesus was Repentance.

The seventh lesson or principle is always the product principle.

What have the Mahatmas brought forth by their religious or philosophical system of thought after so many thousands of years of announcement?

What has Christianity brought forth after 2,000 years of announcement?

The day when the Judgment of man is called to face the products of philosophy or religion or science is the day when the seventh angel is sounding.

The twelve elders on the right hand of the throne of your "I AM" are the twelve law lessons of Moses. They are the strong right arm of the law that terrifies with its rigors. They tell you that he that taketh up the sword must perish by the sword. This was the patience and faith of the saints. All the saints of old believed terribly in the law.

The twelve elders on the left of the throne of your "I AM" are the twelve unlawful lessons of Christ, or the gospel twelve, wherein your sins are blotted out and no matter what your life has been, it is nothing. Christ Jesus is the gospel of discovering that what was already ordained for man is already here, and that which was ordained for him was from the beginning, his own independent, shining soul.

The twelve law lessons are plainly put before us in those Spiritual Science lessons which are called Introductory. The twelve gospel lessons are plainly put in those Spiritual Science lessons which are called Esoteric.

They both fall down when the "I AM" announces itself.

Moses was addressing every department of action. If there is any one principle of thought or conduct to which you have married yourself, you will see a day when the fruits of that marriage will be visible.

Seneca, the Stoic philosopher, urged doing good and thinking nobly without regard to fruits. He did not marry himself to his principle, however, and amassed immense wealth by bribery and defrauding the poor.

Jesus taught that the seeking God first and foremost would be apparent. You could not avoid detecting the actual marriage of your mind to your principles. Whatever line a man works on, he sees the result somewhere, sometime, somehow. "They have their reward." [Matthew 6:2]

"Each tree and herb after its kind, bringeth its fruit, for its seed is in itself." Thus wrote Moses.

If a mind has been attending to outward, material or even intellectual performances, it has been neglecting its Soul fact. To turn and attend entirely to the Soul fact, is to repent. Jesus and John urged attention to the Soul as the Supreme business of man.

This attention must exhibit in beautiful environments, noble conduct, pure speech, lofty powers, daily probity (integrity). It is said of Lord Melbourne that he hated sermons which even hinted that a man's religion and his private daily life were in any way related, while Gladstone complains that sermons do not now lay stress enough upon connection between religious principles and daily conduct. Jesus insisted that certain signs would indicate those who kept his sayings. Their conduct would be noble, gentle, healing, uplifting, generous, unoffending. The fruits of your marriage to your Soul will be the manifestation of Jesus Christ powers, Jesus Christ wisdom, Jesus Christ beauty, Jesus Christ majesty. Jesus Christ authority.

Marriage to your Soul was the subject of the first lesson. Its name was The Word. It has all through the centuries been called The Lost Word, because neither by the law lessons of Moses nor the freedom lessons of Jesus has your own Lost Word been found.

John talks of revealing it. He shows that something like dropping all lessons is the only way for your hidden One, the Lord God Almighty of your being, to be seen on its throne. You have a majestic Authority over the whole universe. Sitting still in your chamber, your thoughts being in your management, you will see your world all easy to conquer. Marriage to your own authority is what Jesus Christ illustrated. He stood among the multitudes and commanded leprosy to depart. He commanded the winds and the sea. He commanded life to appear and death to abscond. They all obeyed Him.

Some contend that there never was any historic Jesus Christ. This does not matter. If the Jesus Christ principle is within us all, it is the one for us to marry unto. "Acquaint now thyself with Me and be at peace." [Job. 22:21]

The man who lives and thinks and talks on the material plane will interpret marriage and bringing forth as material performances. The man who lives and talks and thinks on the intellectual plane will interpret marriage and bringing forth as the sympathy and union of congenial minds. Both are very far from the Jesus Christ type and signification. "In heaven they neither marry nor are given in marriage." [Mark 12:25] Yet He speaks of the marriage of the Lamb. [Revelation 21:9]

The attention of your whole mind and all your senses towards the Jesus Christ point in yourself, is your marriage. This is the only marriage that is real. The rest are all symbols, shadows, dreams, unrealities, phantasmagorias. They may interest you and claim great attention from you, but their fruitage is plain to be seen in the fullness of time. You become a wailing old fool. Not even an Emerson, a Bucher, a Beaconsfield, could escape disclosing to the world to what he had been married.

The Jesus Christ in yourself is Authority over the rot of old age, wrinkles, gray hair, feebleness, fear, competition, child-bearing, school training, warfare, stealing, murder, preaching, missioning, temperance, howling, eating, drinking, sleeping. These all obey your immortal Jesus Christ One at your center, forever on the throne of Authority within your own being. Knowest thou thy Lord?

David caught one glad sight of his own headquarters of his own true throne. He sang, "God will redeem my soul from the power of the grave." [Psalms 49:15]

The Soul is your one name. God is your one name. Understanding is your one name. Mind is your one name. God is a name that David said had power to show you as an authority over death.

A woman in great affliction breathed her whole being full of the Name, God. Suddenly, as by an invisible hand, those afflictions fell away. She reaped the fruits in an instant. The fruits of what? The fruits of attention with all her being, so far as she had got accustomed to enlivening it, to the Divine. She looked not to man, to woman, to things, for help; she looked to God. It is not written, "Call thou upon John Alden in the day of thine adversity and he will deliver thee." It is written, "Call thou upon Me in the day of adversity, and I will deliver thee."

The Divinity, the God, the Soul, the Sight, the Understanding, the Firm Mind, the Jesus Christ Point, has its everlasting throne in yourself.

Coomra Swami told the German traveler that no books, no teachers, no investigations in any direction would disclose to any man what he wanted to know. He would never know, he could never know, anything except by learning from his own soul's wondrous pages, wondrous beams.

The fruits of one glance at your own central fire are soon seen.

Mary saw once. She brought forth Jesus. All other bringing forth is sham—it never took place in reality. Thus it is easy to tell a man who thinks he inherited sores from fathers and mothers in flesh, that he had in reality only One to inherit anything from, and that One is God. [Matthew 23:9]

This puts all the elders to one side. They fall on their faces. All the old religions fall down under this principle. Only the limpid splendor of the undescribed Soul, the Lord God Almighty of your being, is left. (Revelation 1:16-17]

Now, it is seen by this principle how it is not real that; we are placed amid a race of marriages and bringings forth in flesh. We are really placed in God. The rest are but signs, symbols, hints. They are not marriage. The Lamb is your Soul.

Your wonderful life, your heavenly city, your realm of light, is your fruitage. You give yourself to your shining Soul. You are not, that your Soul may be all. Gladly you lie down and disappear forever as anything, that your Real Self may be seen.

Every attention to God has its fruitage. There are some attentions to principles themselves that have been followed by fruitages. They were called paths towards God; towards your own throne of Authority where you sit, judging the twelve powers of your being, sending them forth. Calling them home as Jesus sent His twelve and recalled them again and again.

There is one practice of attention toward absence from theft. The pure absence from theft from your mind was said thousands of years ago to result finally in material wealth. "When absence from theft in mind and action is accomplished in the yogi, he has the power to obtain all material wealth."[11]

Now, it may seem that we, in our enlightened state of society, are quite free indeed from theft in mind as we are in act. But the fruit of this generation is evidence of the great thefts in the people's minds. Was there ever such a state of poverty?

Theft in act is well suppressed by violence and otherwise, but what of theft of mind where it is the

---

[11] This is probably from *How to Know God, the Yoga Aphorisms of Patanjali*, an interpretation of the Hindu *Upanishads* translated by Isherwood and Vivekenanda. [see next note.]

disposition to get something from someone somehow? How are you thinking of getting your honest living? Is it not by taking something from yourself, which is theft, and giving it to someone else, that you may get something from them, which is all a species of mental theft? Why do so, when what is wanted by you is already owned by you and you cannot take it from yourself? David sang of this, that should bless his own Soul, "Men will praise thee when thou doest well to thyself." (Psalms 49:18]

There is no getting from anyone.

There is no giving to anyone.

The desire to give is stealing from your self mentally.

The desire to get is stealing from your neighbor mentally.

The Divinity, your One on His Shining Throne of authority within yourself, desires neither way, therefore, steal not.

The boundless wealth that comes to you by ceasing to desire to do or be done by, by ceasing to desire to give or to get, by ceasing to desire to be praised or to praise, to teach or to be taught, is only an outward symbol of your boundless possessions of Soul. That Divine One on Its throne in yourself that holds onto nothing stretches forth to get nothing. In other words, It steals not. This is taught in that Yogi philosophy as sure fruit or bringing forth from attention to not stealing.

A tedious training. But it is not tedious to attend to your Shining One.

The Yogi have certain pleasant postures which by attending strictly to, there will be a fruitage in feeling no effects from fire and frost, air and no air, breath and no breath. This, they aver, is very difficult to reach. But the seventh insistence of the Jesus Christ Principle within you is. "My yoke is easy, My burden is light, and ye shall find rest unto your Souls." Rest, from central Soul to outer affairs; everything in order.

Yet each of these trees and herbs has its seed in itself. That is, by its own nature, it brings forth something.

There is a teaching in that herby, savory doctrine, of how inaudible mutterings bring one into plain sight of his heart's imagined good. Inaudible mutterings are half-whispered sentences. First, the name of the Supreme One—then the kindness, beauties, wonders of the Supreme One.

The different fruits of the different kinds of attention were arranged in order ages ago by a philosopher whose whole mind had practiced the different trees and grasses of his mind as it was related to his daily lot. His name was Pantajali.[12] But the Divine One, the Absolute and Changeless

---

[12] Pantajali - [c. 4th century, BCE]. Author of Yoga *Sutras* or Aphorisms, called by one translator (Isherwood), *How to Know God*. These are practices, spiritual disciplines and techniques of meditation by which men may achieve a unitive knowledge of the Godhead. Several translations are available.

One, God in you, being attended to, is sure to show these same perfect states without your painful practice of studying any one herb, whether concentrating on a fine point to make your mind sharp; or upon continence to get strength of mind.

Nothing can injure your Divine One. It is your untouchable, unapproachable Soul.

Nothing can advantage your Divine One. It is your untouchable Soul.

All heaven springs forth around you. Bring forth, therefore. It is your sure lot destiny, nature, to bring forth.

How will you bring forth? From attention to the offers that are made you from the different principles which have fruits of different kinds in them? From attention to the One. Moses taught that all were brought forth from God. The earthly splendors flung their happy apples and friendly shelters forth from the Shining Light. That earth had no pain upon it—no curse. All was good. Why? Because there was no Maker mentioned, no Origin alluded to, but One.

The instant any other Origin is mentioned, whether of the mind that by practicing not stealing gets rich, or by the body seeking marriage, there is pain, poverty, despair.

We notice that all the ascetics and priests of spiritual matters have through all ages insisted that in the human marriage there is something ungodly. This is because it is but a symbol of the completeness of the One that neither marries nor is given in marriage. In the human desire of union there is the theft thought of wanting to get and to give. The Truth of each one is that they need nothing and need give nothing. In spiritual matters, there is always the fruitage of desires stopped. The one wish that remains in your heart is the one theft of your mind that shows as poverty of some kind. A blank place in your lot shows that one theft. Desire is the only theft.

Fullness of all life comes with absence of desires. But absence of desire was never managed by anyone while he was trying to get rid of desire. Looking at the desireless One, all desires fall away. The pure in heart see God. Desire has always been termed impurity. The desireless one faces God. This brings forth fullness, completeness. Nothing is wanting. All is fed life, satisfied

There is always one cure in Christian healing that stands forth as the sign that you have given up believing in matter as a reality. Always some good miracle happens when you have given up depending on anyone for your happiness.

There is always some cure that happens for giving up believing in the power of pain.

There is one cure happens, as Pantajali said, for believing God has given you exactly as much as all others have. There is one cure happens for believing that you are a Divine Being vested with Divine Powers.

There is a miracle sure to happen if you remember that your Divinity is able to lift you out of the garbage of crying, debt, fickle friendships, poor luck.

But all the miracles of all the ages and all the principles are the swift bringing forth of knowing that there is only the Divine One whose throne is your own Divine Authority.

VIII

TRUTH

"And God said. Let there be lights in the firmament of the heavens." [Genesis 1:14]

"And the nations were angry, and thy wrath is come, and the time of the dead, that they should be judged, and that thou shouldst give reward unto thy servants and prophets and to the saints, and them that fear thy Name, small and great; and shouldst destroy them which destroy the earth." [Revelation 11:18]

The Divine in man, in yourself, is not heard speaking as a human voice, yet it is as plainly understood by you when listened for by you, as any human voice could be. It is not in sound like the clap of the tongue and lips on the airs, but it seems rather like a distinct sentence of your Bible or favorite book that comes to you.

If you are greatly absorbed in your daily human lot, the sentence that strikes your mind will not be heard by you as original, unprecedented information, but rather, like a poorly rendered quotation from a book. Try to remember how your mind has carried that line of poetry and it will be clear to you that you have not had it as the author wrote it.

The voice of God is perpetually speaking to you. If you hear it as some sudden text of your memory, that is the lens through which you have viewed the never- ceasing voice. It is your light. Let it remain with you and be obedient to it. Scorn it not. It was by poor lenses they first saw the moons of Mars, the belts of Saturn, the spots on the Sun. "I turned to see the voice," said John. So the use of a poor lens leads to finding a better one.

Turning to see a voice exactly expresses the sensation of direction or information from Spirit. If you are in perplexity, ask the present God which way to turn. Soon you may hear a text in your mind. It may be, "I will show thee." Now, the text as it was read in your youth may have been: "I will lead thee by a way that thou hast not known," but the way it now comes to you is your lens.

If you had been listening to that voice every moment of your life and had not been so absorbed in your cares, you would have heard the voice as plainly as Peter heard it say, "Rise. Peter, gird on thy cloak." You might have heard it say. "Go to the garret and examine the brass box." For the directions on the human pathway are all speaking plainly concerning every action, every moment.

Clear light on all pathways is so possible that there are no pathways at all. You have found your home. Moses knew the voice of the Divine Presence as well as he knew the voice of his wife.

This text concerning the lights is now plain. Let all the directions now be plainly heard by you. If you are much in human turmoil, that is darkness, but even there you have stars and moonlight. They are those answers that come straight.

If it seems as if you were led to go in and see a minister of the gospel, go and see him. If he spurn you and your turmoil, that is not the point. The point is you were true to all the light you had. That was the peculiarity of Abraham. He said, "Yea" to every direction his mind seemed to suddenly catch. Thus, he finally came to have bold clear lights on his path—bold, clear, unmistakable lights. This voice that Moses heard showing how creation proceeds, was the same voice that he heard saying, "My presence shall go with thee, and I will give thee rest." [Exodus 33:14]

Thus, lights are informations. Informations may be clear and definite, coming through a lens that is not distracted or half obscured by our intense wills. The eager desire for anything obscures that mental perception which may be called hearing or seeing. God, the Supreme One, is desireless. Therefore, the nearer desireless we are, the less obscured our lens or mind's hearing. In the mind, you will discover that hearing and sight are the same. The mind's perception is not in symbol at its clearest, but in clear knowledge.

To see a star as a symbol to keep on the way we are going, is symbol. To know by the swift knowledge that makes it seem like actual words, is not symbol—except to God—the Supreme One who knows no words.

Set your mind firm in its first principles; take all the informations that come. Then let your mind, at its wisdom point, detect the Truth best for yourself. This is receiving the lights. Attending to this eighth advice of Moses as coming from his Lord, there would never be any wars, or commerce, or traveling. Man would find all knowledge, all peace, all bliss, staying at his home point and letting the Universe teach him the meaning of each thing.

The mind that receives Truth from the stones is kind to the stones and they are kind to him. The man and the stones understand each other. The stone shines and smiles with information for man. The savage of the desert who wanted to kill you does nothing but show you his soul's light.

He who beholds the One Light in all forms, lets forms remain. They all tell him of One Light. They all tell him each its own tale. And light is life. So man need not seek in his world for his subsistence, for his world by the light gives him life. "Because I live, ye shall live also."

Coomra Swami told Hensoldt[13] that no man ever knew anything by seeking first without himself. He must know how to interrogate himself as Moses did, before the outer universe would disclose its meaning, its informations, its lights, to him.

There is one set of Vedas, or Oriental lessons of the Divine one, that shows how each mind, by noticing the Light that is always shining toward it, becomes illuminated and draws the illumination point from all things.

This set of lessons explains that all looking away from that Light which is the shining knowledge on the mind, by asking for God, is delusion. Everything we behold in nature is delusion. Everything we behold in man is delusion. Nothing is real but the point of Light. And each point of Light has a voice. But that voice is, in its clearest shining, never a message about matter, or conduct, or activity, or prosperity, or misery. Its voice is like nothing but Itself. Yet listening to it without seeing it, asking for direction of an unseen Knower, lo, it sounds like a voice telling us which ship to sail in, or which broom to sweep with.

---

[13] Hensoldt was a German adventurer who visited India in the late 1800s and shared the results of his interviews and initiatory trainings in a series of articles and books.

The lens through which we perceive the Light is obscured by knowledge of matter and action. Knowledge of matter and action is not Knowledge. Matter is not reality, and the actions of matter are delusions. The Light that shines from them is what is real. Let the mind drop its knowledge of matter and actions and the true Light will shine. Drop knowledge to have Knowledge.

Descartes[14] found that his schoolbook knowledge obscured his own native Light He practiced not knowing, that he might know. Thus he discovered his own Light.

The One Divine Sun that shines is shining everywhere, through all things; but there is a common consent through the ages of man's listening for the voice of direction on his path, that man first must know his own Self. The more a man knows of his own Light, the more he knows of the Light of information in all things. At one point of his knowledge there is but one light, and he himself is that Light.

---

[14] René Descartes is the 17th century philosopher who said "*Cogito ergo sum* (I think, therefore I am)" and found a way to remove science from under control of the Roman Church by separating all things mental and spiritual (the realm of the Church) from all things material (the realm of Science), a separation usually called "the Cartesian split."

Lao Tze taught that there is but one *Tao*.[15] There is one nourisher of the Light of *Tao*. That is *Te*, or virtue. There is one manifestation of *Tao*. That is the King, the Original Light, the Lover of Light, the Manifester of the Light. Therefore, the only book he thought would express this lesson should be called *Tao-Te-King*.

That Light that is the Original One was called "The Abysmal Nothing" by Jacob Boehme.[16] That Light from which sprang all things and which is shining through all things was called "The Divine Dark" by Tauler. It was called "The One Substance" by Spinoza. It was called "The Unconditioned Absolute" by Kant.[17] It was called "The Unknowable" by the Brahmins and Buddhists. Even Spencer calls it "The Unknowable."

But our Bible calls it "The Light." Our Bible points to its meeting man on every plane of his being and shining a help onward for him. His health is told in its Voice and the way for him to be wholesomely beautiful forever. His prosperity is

---

[15] 'Lao-Tzu [b. 604 B.C.E; China]-Founder of system of religion known as Taoism — a "creative quietism" through which man seeks inner accord with the conscience of the universe. Author of what is known today as the *Tao Te Ching*, a collection of 81 poems. [*Tao* = the way of all life; *Te* = the fit use of life by men; *Ching* = a text or classic] There are many translations available.

[16] Boehme, Jacob - German mystic and philosopher - [1575-1624]; *The Way of Christ* Treatise 7, Ch. 2,120.

[17] Kant Immanuel - German Philosopher - [1724 -1804]; *Critique of Pure Reason.* Book II, Ch. Ill, § 3, p. 276.

told in its Voice and the way to be safely prosperous forever.

The Voice, when listened to, shows man that prosperity is not dependent upon money or no money, favor of rich men or poor men. Prosperity is of the Light—the informing Light.

Health is in its Voice and man finds his health not dependent upon eating sleeping, upon liniments and cordials. Health is of the Lord, the miracle-working Light. An old man in Jersey City was in a painful state of disease. His wife offered him a glass of water to revive him. "Nay, I do not need it the Lord will cure me." he said. Within five minutes he was utterly cured He let the Light break into his mind and speech.

James found people praying for money with which to make themselves rich and honored. He saw that there was no Light in such a state of mind. He called it lust. He showed that the Lord never struck through them with the prospered Light so that a miracle was wrought for them. They had to go to work in the world's fashion, for their prayer was on that plane. A miracle of assistance from a direction not wrought out by your exertions, is a rift from a higher plane. The higher the plane the help comes from, the farther we get from desire, from darkness, from matter, from delusion, from conditions and actions of the physical. The outward passions which need good sensations must go to work outwardly to get their prayers answered.

The *Bhagavad-Gita*[18] says, "Actions can only produce actions as animal produce their kind." The mind that looks for wisdom and yet thinks whether the bed is hard or soft, the meat hot or cold, the drink strong or weak, gets its own wisdom by thinking sublime truths.

The mind that knows that its thoughts are not God, stops thinking gladly, and lets the Supreme One move Itself over his still waters. Moses explained it as God moving over the face of the waters. The mind that is not mind any more, being lost at sight of God, the Supreme Light, sees light everywhere, and is a miracle worker by his presence anywhere. Instantly, the poor man shows bounty to him. He is the harmless one. Abraham read the light as a message to slay. Obedience to it showed it in a clearer Voice.

Mahomet/Mohammed heard the Voice as direction to slay. Not noticing the stronger Voice of mercy and loving gentleness, he slew thousands upon thousands, and the darkness of epilepsy seized him. Hugging the darkness and not heeding the Light, he was finally poisoned to death. He lived on a plane where he caught messages from a plane nearer mercy, harmlessness, desirelessness, but would not receive these messages from above.

[18] *Bhagavad-Gita, The Song of God,* The most popular book in Hindu religious literature, from the 5th to 2nd centuries, B.C. It is a gospel in that its essential message is timeless: incarnate God speaks to man, His friend. The classic translation is by Swami Prabhavananda & Christopher Isherwood, Vedanta Press, Hollywood, CA, 1944.

We are all hearing voices from the Light, as it shines on our path; action and endeavor if we live on that plane; miracles if we take our new thoughts; wonderful illuminations when we dwell beyond thoughts. Even the stones shine with messages. Even the snakes shine with directions. The heart is wise and shining. Yea, the very heart in your bosom. Call it not matter. Its smile is the shine of the Divine One whose Name has been called Spirit.

John said (in Revelation 11:18) that the nations were angry, for the wrath of God had come. The nations on the material plane are like Martha scolding Mary for not acting vigorously. The people on the mind plane are insisting we must exercise our thoughts. The people who think nothing, but watch the ever-shining Light, are certain the rest are wrong.

Whatever plane you are on, say nothing against any other man's methods. He will have Light on his way. Let his Light be praised. John said the time of judging had come, for the saints and the prophets. That is true. Do we not now know on which plane they lived and taught? That is our judgment.

Then again, John said, now is the time when those should be destroyed who destroyed the earth. Is it not a destruction of action, endeavor, competition to know that it is no help to knowing the Voice of the Light?

Is it not a destroyer of thinking, to know that by thinking nothing, comes the Light straight to the Light within us?

But is it not the sure Presence of the Light when every sense within us knows all about the Light? Is it not the Presence of the Light that needs no sun to symbolize itself, when we know all things and need not that any man should teach us?

The true Light shines at the central point of all things. That is why all things have their names and their habits on every plane. The tree has a habit of covering itself with split barks. The vines have a habit of trailing. The very rheumatism in your shoulder has a twinge that is not the twinge of anything else. These all tell the wonderful story of the God that charges them.

If you take the story different from its meaning, you are deceived. "Be not deceived," said Jesus. Judas was always taking the stories of the good pervertedly. Therefore, he hanged himself. Afterward, Matthias took his place. Judas stood for intellect, which often finds the answers of the Spirit impossible to understand. Matthias is intellect that bows its head knowing that the answer is clear and right even if it cannot comprehend it. The intellect cannot do anything but think and think over words and sentences. It turns them to suit itself. The body moving by its senses, perishes. The intellect moving by its thoughts, perishes.

Mind and body acknowledging the unperishing One are soon bathed with Life—with Light.

Mind does not control the body. Judas tore open his body [Acts 1:18]. Mind tells how tired it is and tells of its perishing body. Mind dissects animals, plants, stones, bones, and determines their names and laws. Then mind wonders at the changes and fadings of all things. Mind calls it analysis of matter, "knowledge"; but there is only one knowledge. That is the knowledge of God.

"The natural mind receiveth not the things of the Spirit." The intellect receiveth not God. It has to bow down and call God "Unknowable." But the Self in man knows God. For itself is the God.

The physician, Luke, who wrote the 3rd Gospel and also wrote the "Acts of the Apostles," was always addressing the god chord in man. He called it "O Theophilus."[19] Let all that you say, O people—let all that you say, O reader—be addressed while you are alone, to your God chord, your Theophilus. Let all that you say be addressed to the God chord in your neighbor. So shall healing spring forth. So shall Light break forth. Keep touching the God chord in all things. Keep it up. Wait for their responses.

A lady had a habit of asking the door to her drawing room if anyone were coming. It had a way

---

[19] The name *Theophilus,* combines two Greek words: *Theos* (meaning God) and *Philos* (meaning Love), so it may be translated as "God-Lover."

of informing her. This was her plane of action. She was asking it of material things. If her heart leaped, she knew some dear friend was coming.

"Be not deceived," said Jesus. "Believe in God." "Believe in Me."

The God smiling through that door will tell her some new truth. Well for her if she receive it. The God springing and shining through her heart will tell her some new truth. That which is coming will not pretend to matter. It will tell of the Supreme Spirit. Maybe its message may be to her that she must now cease from being made unhappy by false friends. She must have herself to be her friend. "Thy Maker is thy Husband." If she gets that message, she may let its Light guide her mind to indifference to pleasant comrades and indifference to painful accusations. The human mind cannot receive this true Light. It is too bright. So the human mind must acquiesce cheerily. "Very well," let it say.

All the friendships of the world are delusions. The One in man that is Friend, dies not, departs not, changes not.

If one with a strong will so chooses, he can hide your mind and eyesight so that they will not see any friend or foe though they might be in the same room. This is hypnotism. It is mesmerism. It is deception. It is delusion.

It was some strong will that said death stole my child.[20] It was the will of the opposite of God. Its name is devil. Its name is prince of this world. Its name is lie. Its name is nothingness.

Watch the cat call the bird. See the bird look and flutter, trying to fly. How oppressed its wings! How pitiful its peep! Tell it to fly. Tell it that it has wings. You will see it lift its wings and fly free.

Watch the world's deception calling man to die, to be poor, to be old, to be friendless, to be looking forward to something to come—he knows not what. Tell him he is free, wise, immortal. Tell him he is Spirit-Supreme Spirit You are addressing his Self. The hiding world delusion cannot stay where your Truth goes mixing with it, cutting through it. Something in the world shadow, the world hypnotism, the world deceptiveness, cannot bear Truth. "Truth is Lord over all." Truth cannot be conquered, but everything falls which opposes it, while all that is like it shines forth.

See how the cat hypnotism falters when you tell the bird it has wings. Even cat hypnotism falters at a simple truth. Now, see how earth hypnotism falters when at the bedside of your friend, you tell him he is alive forevermore. See how the earth deceptiveness falters when you tell the woman or the man they are cheerfully perfect forevermore.

---

[20] Emma Hopkins' son, her only child, is recorded as having died in his 20s.

Could the earth influences falter, if they had any Substance, Intelligence, Reality in them? Reality is the changeless, eternal God. Unreality is the varying change—not God.

Whenever any power seems to be operating with strength against anyone, tell him the Truth. Deny the world belts as Jesus denied them. Standing in the midst of the multitude, He called the Divinity in even the Judases, His mother and His brethren. Speaking of the children of Light, He said that those who were in the world's claims could not even by the most enchanting influences cause them to rejoice or weep.

IX

HOLINESS

"And God said, Let the waters bring forth abundantly." [Genesis 1:20]

"And the temple of God was opened in heaven." [Revelation 11:19]

"Waters" are freely moving graces. The thief on the cross opened a gate and forthwith the free grace of God came flowing and he had all paradise.

The temple of God is man. "Know ye not that ye are the temple?" asked Paul [I Corinthians 3:16]. When a man turns his eyes up and backwards, he beholds the Kingdom of Heaven in himself. "The Kingdom of Heaven is within you."

If you take notice of the eyes of an artist or an author, they always look up and backwards with a mysterious light. This is their unconscious turning toward that Kingdom of Heaven within themselves which any man who consciously or unconsciously gets a glimpse of, will find to be a well of inspiration.

"Whatsoever things ye desire," oh, man, dip your cup into your own Kingdom of Heaven. Then come the splendid fires of genius in words of Truth that set the world agog. From them drip the sparkles of Light that teach the painter everything.

The musician dips his hearing in the waters that fall from heaven and they sound to human ears most ravishing.

The whole Bible is given over to calling man's attention to looking-beholding-gazing-watching-considering WHAT? Always one thing, viz: the Kingdom of Heaven—God—Jesus Christ—the Lamb WHERE? Within you!

All geniuses have looked backward and upward toward this Kingdom from whence they all came out. In that country, we had all beauty. It lies at hand—just back of us. We have ability of mind, inner turning power, to look into that Kingdom steadfastly, beholding the living streams till we dip again into our first estate of beauty, strength, inspiration.

With every breath drawn from out our Kingdom, there is enchantment With every breath we spread abroad from partaking of that breath; we are a joy to our world.

"Look unto Me"—unto whom? The Lamb in the midst of you that shall lead you into free ways, into the happy lands of daily experience Moses saw the living creatures moving from the opening of gates that let the waters flow. Wells of water flowing forth in streams from heaven The names of the Kingdom of God in me are many. But none of them has such an open sesame in its sound as Jesus Christ, because all the names of God have different sounds, carry different qualities, but that Name is all the fullness of the Godhead bodily. That Name is the Name which John saw on the Isle of Patmos as the one Name that would open the Kingdom of God to you if you would only learn to look backward toward your own starting point and upward into your own place.

Then if you cannot feel or see the gift of looking as the Scriptures declare, you may soon get your eyes set that way by repeating the Name, Jesus Christ. John's Revelation is full of this principle. Moses sees it as the flowing water. Jesus Christ of Nazareth declared that from His abode within us all. He would be flowing, springing water of everlasting life.

After the judgment, all is past. The judgment is the joy of mankind, not their sorrow. Jesus Christ is the living judgment in you, whereby you are awake, alive, spiritually on fire, so that when all that is your perfect judgment is arisen, can you not see that there will be no good and evil to judge between?

In Oriental philosophy, taught by the sages of India, there is the doctrine of the Absolute and Eternal One having distributed Himself through all space in order to enjoy Himself. And this accounts for the chaos of this universe, looking as if it were a broken and distributed mass of particles which were once united.

The distribution of God, the Unnamable One, is called by them, "*Manvantara.*"[21] They teach that the Absolute One is now drawing Himself together again. He will soon be all in one Point. This they call "*Pralaya.*"[22] Now, while God is spread abroad and scattered, it is called by them, "God's day." When He draws Himself together into one Point again, it is called, "God's night," because then He rests.

By this philosophy, we would have to say that the first chapter of Genesis was God's drawing Himself together from the chaos, because it ends with the rest of God.

---

[21] *Manvantara* (also *Samsara)* that period of life and activity between [that which] initiates the evolution of all thinking forms at the dawn of manifestation, and [that which] remains at the close of manifestation. [*Sanskrit Keys to the Wisdom Religion.* Judith M. Tyberg, Point Loma Publications, Inc., San Diego, CA, 1976, p. 29.]

[22] *Pralava* (also *Pahlevi)-* Just as dissolution implies a transformation of substances into another state of matter, so at the time of Pralaya, all manifested or visible things dissolve or vanish into the nominal or invisible worlds: the Many return to their Source, become the ONE. [Ibid, p. 30]

The rest of God is when He had drawn all the intelligence of all-all worlds—all-all space, all-all sentience—together.

The activity of God is the chaos that preceded our man type. Long before man could be formulated, the Mighty One had made chaos of Himself. Now, in returning to Himself, man is His crowning creation. At the ninth stage, the return is God calling the flowing mind to make joys, loves, harmonies, friendly feelings. Let them come flowing together to be finally all one in man. One man shall embody them all. One man shall be the acme of drawing together before the final rest. Then God shall multiply and replenish and redistribute Himself again in a new fashion not at all like this one.

Ages upon ages of watching God have given the Brahmins and Buddhists this conviction. If we show them the book of Genesis, they see it as God calling Himself together again after distributing Himself, and His last, last moment is rest. The night is *Pralaya.*

There is something very majestic in this interpretation of the proceedings of the universe. Take notice of one thing, namely, that it is very like the atomic theory of our European world thinkers. Spencer and Tyndall say that atoms once distributed are hurrying to unite themselves together again. They call atoms matter. The Eastern philosophers call it Spirit. But when all things are united into one, there can be neither Spirit nor matter, for these are pairs of opposites. If you mention Spirit, you mean an opposite to matter. If you mention matter, you mean an opposite to Spirit. As the Spirit is God over matter-ruler over it, so when there is no matter to rule over, then the office of Spirit is finished and there is no Spirit. What is left? The Unspeakable. Moses calls it rest. Jesus Christ called it the New Name.

The heavenly kingdom is full of health, full of life, full of genius. Look into it and let it give you what you please. Whatsoever things ye ask for, ye shall have. Nothing is too material. One element is not more spiritual than another.

The thoughts of your mind are far from God when they are saying, "God," for the word. "God," is not the Name. If you should be looking into your kingdom of heaven, you would there find that the Name is not "God" any more than it is chair. The name you enter with is the wish you dip in with. That which you bring forward is joy, harmony. Its name is not joy, but its gift is joy.

Grace. The disciples were materially-minded fishermen. They got their living by fishing. They were on Galilee, which means circuit. They were called to preach the law of the word. They preached it. They were again on the lake. They were called to the good word, the law of the good only. They preached it. They felt it. This was law. They got their living by preaching, teaching, healing. Jesus was now absent. They were again on the circuit lake. Again they were called. This time they found their bread and fish prepared, but they were free gifts. All their preaching, teaching, healing, counted nothing. Their fishing, practicing, was not their living. God was their provider. They had the same kind of food and protection, but it was not provided in the usual way.

The whole teaching of Jesus Christ concerns the harmonious providing unity between the Kingdom of Heaven and the world through which we journey. Milton wrote: "What if the earth be but the shadow of heaven, and things thereon, each unto each more like than on earth is seen?"

Why should a man kill animals for his food? Why should we labor and strive, and then some of us get no clothes and others of us get comfortable ones? Why, with all their struggles, are some cold and starved while others are comforted? Does not that show that the system is all wrong? How does it happen that a man who makes guns, if he makes those that kill most men, is accounted greatest? And the man who kills most cattle is greatest, also? Do not our great magazines praise and portray as our greatest men, those who kill most?

Dipping into the Kingdom of Heaven, we draw gentleness, mercy, genius, beauty, gladness. There is no death there; there is no night there; there is no sorrow there. But though the joys and splendors of heaven are ours, there are distant researches in that direction which touch beyond even our highest joys. "It hath not entered into the mind of man" to conceive of that heaven as it is.

Our first move is to remember our God-point— our starting Point. This turns our eyes upward and backward like Mary's in the picture of the Immaculate Conception.[23] Conception is an idea. An immaculate conception is an idea not mixed with words or thoughts. We are capable of such a concept—such an idea.

Our second move is to behold how this vision of the Divine Point within us dissolves obstacles softly, gently, no fuss, no noise, no excitement but all disadvantages count for nothing. They fall away.

The third move is testing that we are the One ourselves. This is identification, agreement with our Adversary. There is only one adversary in the realm of Light and Life, and that is God. "Behold, I am against thee, saith the Lord."

We tell the Almighty One what is in our secret hearts. This does not convince the Almighty Adversary, but we become joyously convinced. Our cup runneth over.

Though Daniel was a strong metaphysician, so strong that with his mind he could undo the work of the Chaldean magicians, and so strong that he

---

[23] The picture she's describing is, rather, *The Annunciation.* In the tradition of the Roman Church, the Immaculate Conception describes the conception of Mary, Mother of Jesus, who must be born sinless if she is to bear God's Son, rather than the conception of Jesus in Mary by the Holy Spirit.

could work greater miracles than Elijah or Solomon, yet his heart was filled with grief. So he told his Adversary, the High and Holy One that inhabiteth eternity, all about it. This relieved him of grief. The free draft of Holy Wind blew through him. He was filled with skill and understanding. This was harmony with the Adversary. Agreement. Then he was full of prophecies for our own age of the world. We can see about where we stand in the coming events of time by reading Daniel.

With the judgment angels, the end of time arrives. John saw an angel with one foot on the sea and one on the land, proclaiming that time should be no more. Time is ended. No more reckoning.

Calculating, counting, reckoning are all Judas transactions. Judas found his end. Mind that reckons, splits itself. The gift of God, [which is the meaning of] Matthais,[24] is better than calculating. When you go to treat your affairs to make them lay themselves out in beautiful order, you find them already fixed. Time, with its intellectual task of thinking affairs into order, is done away with - ended. The miracle is wrought for you. This is Free Grace—Rest.

The effort of thinking is part of the curse. John heard the angel say, "There shall be no more curse." Under cause and effect, the curse is effect. Under Free Grace, rest.

---

[24] Matthias, or Matthew, was appointed one of the 12 disciples to replace Judas Iscariot.

Intellect tells over and over what it wants done; tells how it all ought to be done; age in and age out. But inspiration, the free Wind of God blowing through the mind, dissolves the mind's whole shroud, and lo, there is no mind. As long as we keep the name Mind as a name of God, we shall have thinking; as long as we keep the name God, we shall have governing and ruling, superiority and inferiority. The name of the High and Holy One that inhabiteth eternity is not God.

As long as we have the word, "Lord," for a name of the Almighty, the One Most High, we shall have helping and healing and blessing.

There is no helping, healing, blessing, after judgment of mind is set.

When mind has good judgment, it decides against there being any mind. When mind has thus set itself aside into the realm of nowhere, the reign of the City of God where men know nothing is here in our midst.

It is far better to know nothing than something. God knows nothing.

Should things occupy the Unnamable One who is not a thinker?

X

FORGIVENESS

"And God said: Let the earth bring forth the living creature after his kind, cattle and creeping things." [Genesis 1:24]

"And the nations were angry, and Thy wrath is come, and the time of the dead that they should be judged, and that THOU shouldst give reward unto thy servants." [Revelation 11:18]

"Earth" is rounded whole, all I am. The God quality in me says a few things in its own tongue perpetually. If I listen as a Moses, I speak with my tongue audibly and it sounds like this text [Genesis 1:24] when I come to talk of the round earth and my relation to it. For I am not able to see cattle and creeping things except I let them be seen. I have certain qualities within me which extend by fine wires outwardly and at the tip end of those wires that go forth from me, I must see cattle; if I extend another set of qualities, at the tip ends thereof I see men.

All things proceed forth from me which I see anywhere. There is, therefore, here at my headquarters a power to transform those cattle and creeping things into angels, into mountains, into anything. The power stands here at my headquarters.

There is one voice in me that Moses called "God." It is the urging voice. It wants to keep me pushing out my wires all the time and making new things to look at. Sometimes this voice has no kind of judgment, for it urges me to make rules and regulations that are as burdensome and irksome to myself as for those creatures at the end of the fine wires. For instance, this urging voice said, "Keep on multiplying and replenishing everything." But I do not want to multiply and replenish the things called cattle and creeping things! I want to abolish that kind of visibility. Even if Moses, my tongue of interpretation, calls these things symbols, I do not want them multiplied. Even if cattle and earth mean solid friends and prosperous affairs, like Joseph in Genesis. I do not want them. What I do want is to cease from this projecting fine wires from my headquarters and having an eternal round of people and affairs to meet.

The tongue that I have let get the sway in my headquarters is Moses. If I do not cease from this host of creatures at the end of my fine wires, I am like the king in the fable who set a fool on the throne in his place, and of course, the fool was king. The true king had abdicated. How should he get this throne back again? So I, if I let the Moses tongue get to describing the God in me, will keep on dealing with an urging God all the time.

It is not till I strike the tongue called Jesus Christ that I see any way to stop the cattle and creeping business and extend from my throne a kind of people and environment that I, myself, want to see.

The Jesus Christ Name is the secret tongue, but if sounded upon constantly it becomes the loud tongue. Moses is all hushed. The Jesus Christ tongue in me starts up with my uttering the Name over and over. This makes the nations appear to be angry. They rise and up heave and stir and splash. This is because the fine wires out from which they project forth from me are being withdrawn. Jesus Christ is not Moses. The Name hushes the projecting sounds and calls them home for me. I am for the first time feeling something like rest from the Moses tongue.

The Jesus Christ tongue which stops the multiplying and replenishing of cattle, men, strange actions and worlds has an undertone. That undertone comes into prominence as I proceed to let the Jesus Christ Name and doctrine stop the old law of things. It is a still more powerful tongue than the name Jesus Christ. John, the Revelator, called it a New Name.

But the Jesus Christ Name is the new king I set on the throne to put down the material set of sights that confront me. There is no urging God in Jesus Christ administration. I hear only one tone forever, and that is not urging my storage of tongues to shoot any wires forward into a world with any creations at their tip ends. That Name is a drawing power for those tongues that, like fools, or like sensible beings, are still eager to get the upper hand in my kingdom.

No name is such a Swallower-up in kindness as this Name. I have noticed that the Moses name never had any kindness in its projecting prowesses. It talked of laws of good and laws of evil continually. The Name of Jesus Christ causes all things to insist on being good in my sight or dying at once. But it is certain that the Name that is under Jesus Christ, the soft, unheard tone, is not speaking of either good or evil. It tells something beyond, sweeter, than the story of the good. As the name Jesus Christ swallowed up all the things the Moses tongue had projected, so the unheard, soft Name swallows up all that the Name Jesus Christ has manifested.

In this clothing of tongues that I have folded myself with, I will let the Name softer than the name Jesus Christ reign. As I take note of the Name that is softer and finer than the name Jesus Christ, I find myself no longer looking outward and forward, no longer throwing ideas outward over a planet to change conditions, but find all the fine wires brought home to my throne. He that sitteth on the throne is in charge of all the creations projected by the Moses name, and also in charge of all the creations projected by the Jesus Christ name. They are all brought into His fingers. The time of the dead is come. It is rest.

All the thoughts, all the feelings, all the senses, are now drawn inward backward, upward, and are in the Name that has its sound under the name Jesus Christ.

This withdrawing, this bringing home, is the real doctrine preached by Jesus of Nazareth. He was a voice teaching repentance. Repentance does not mean wickedness. It means stopping and retracing. All the masterpieces of genius that the world has ever seen were wrought in moments when men suddenly stopped and ceased from looking forward and outward, even with their eyes, and let all their faculties gaze backward and upward to Him that sitteth forever in soft unheard verity on the throne of every man's own being.

There is one common Point in me which is the common Point in all mankind, from whose silent mystery all wonderful, beautiful, majestic things had their origin. Whoever even approximately hints at turning to that Point gets for his substance the genius quality. He makes, like Raphael, divine paintings. Or he makes, like Beethoven, divine music. Or he makes, like Lao Tse, divine paragraphs. Or he makes, like Keeley, a mysterious airship. Or he makes, like Gassner, Divine healings. No wonder Jesus taught for His principle, repentance.

No wonder it was promised to the Israelites that in returning and rest should they be saved. For to turn into the Me of myself is to return to my home throne no matter which of my thoughts I draw home. The Moses tongue has, therefore, driven all the other tongues with its urging to create good objects with shadows of themselves called bad objects. But the Jesus Christ tongue soon draws them all home here to my throne where in soft, unspeaking splendor, the tongue that is the only expresser of me, sitteth hidden forever and ever unless I say its Name and tell it to reign.

John saw this One so long hidden, coming into sight by his looking inward, backward, upward, and heard it say, "Behold I make all things new."

This is the only lesson Jesus Christ taught. He sometimes called it: "Look." He sometimes called it: "Behold." He sometimes called it: "Turn." He sometimes called it: "Repent." He sometimes called it: "consider." Whoever catches himself looking within, backward, upward, catches himself bringing forth new demonstrations.

Solomon told every man that had leisure to watch a little ant. He would find that it would open like a little drop of water and show a multitude of ideas to a man's brain. "Go to the ant, thou sluggard, consider her ways and be wise"

Jesus taught watching birds for bread. He taught watching flowers for clothing. His one wonderful lesson was, "Watch." He knew that to watch anything would be to turn the vision backward and above from whose throne all things come forth.

To get home—to get home here to the throne of me—is my rest. "In returning and rest ye shall be saved." [Isaiah 30:15]

"Learn of Me." The "Me" is my soft voice, the under-key of the name Jesus Christ. It has a manna[25] for my mind so that my mind is brilliantly wise. It has a manna for my tongue so that my tongue is brilliantly true and wise. It has a manna for my body so that my body is well fed and transcendently beautiful.

How wonderful is my world, fed by the manna of that soft Name hidden under the name Jesus Christ.

How gladly all the fine wires draw themselves back, repent, and come home to the throne of the "Me" to be taught how to move. How gladly Moses comes up to "Me" that is the undertone, the unspoken invisible one on the throne here in myself!

---

[25] *Manna* is the foodstuff that the Israelites found in the desert every morning during their Exodus journey in the wilderness.

John beheld it. He heard it speak. Its voice was like no sound he had ever heard before. Its face was like no other face he had ever seen. It said, "Behold, I make all things new."

There is no such thing as poverty at the tip ends of the fine wires that run from this tongue. "They hunger no more, neither thirst any more."

There is poverty with the Moses tongue. There is delay with the Jesus tongue. But with the tongue of the New Name, there is no time. All is true and unspeakably well now. There are no changes to be made.

No one has to trust in this Name or in this Kingdom, hoping for something different to transpire. Nothing different is wanted. All that is, is right. "Thy word is settled in heaven," saith David.

"We go no more out forever," said the Voice to John, speaking for this world

Every treatment sent forth has moth and rust to meet. Even the Name Jesus Christ shot forward into any man will meet so much moth and rust of opposition in him that he is apt to die at once.

The coming backward and inward, homeward here, to my throne, up on high where the Mystic One called the "Lamb" sits, is a highway over which health. strength, wisdom, may walk down to man and make his world beautiful for him with peace and good will -over which the kingdoms of man are drawn back into the throne and thus the kingdoms of this world become the kingdoms of our Lord and His Christ. In Truth, the kingdoms of this world come from their places back, up, into heaven over the lines made by all my faculties turning backward, inward, upward, and beholding Him that sitteth now on my throne.

XI

WISDOM

"And God said, Let us make man in our image, after our likeness; and let them have dominion."
[Genesis 1 :26]

"And the temple of God was opened in heaven and there was seen in his temple the ark of his testament." [Revelation 11:19]

"The eleventh a jacinth." [Revelation 21:20]

Plato saw mankind all looking at shadows on a cave wall. They could not see the real objects till they should wrench themselves around and see behind them.

All the changeable, unreliable situations of human life are those shadows. God, the changeless and eternal Substance, changes and fades not. But all the movements of God, the Eternal, are pictured as nature with its death, change, and unreliability. Images and likenesses are not realities. The instant we turn from likenesses in a mirror, we see the objects that cast them. So when we turn around from beholding what is before our vision, we begin to behold realities. This is repentance.

The vision of man is double. It can see materiality which is image; or it can see Spirituality which is Substance.

The single-eyed see determinedly one-way. When eyes are fixed on matter, they do not see Spirit. When eyes are fixed on Spirit, they do not see matter. "If thine eye be single to Spirit, thy whole body shall be full of light."

To say this to mankind seems absurd, but if mankind stops to consider what has happened around them since they can remember, they will recall that all the wonderful things they have ever done were done because they had not been looking forward, but backward. It is not a difficult thing to do. Close the eyes and throw the vision backward, inward, upward.

Vieta, the mathematician, would spend whole days seeing nothing outside and around himself. His eyes outwardly looked dazed, but his whole vision was engaged mystically. He would then bring forth accurate mathematical solutions.

Archimedes[26] was too engrossed with his background visions to perceive when his life was being threatened by the swords of the Syracuse soldiers.

Jesus was so engaged with the vision of heaven, that for the sake of a world's happiness, He ignored the shame and the pain of a cross. How could images, pictures, delusions, shadows, affect the single-eyed Jesus, the single-eyed Vieta, the single-eyed Archimedes?

Stephen, also, was gazing into the heaven and felt not the stones. That which is discovered by gazing inward and backward and upward is heavenly. "Turn ye turn ye. for why will ye die"? That is, why should you be identified with shadows that end?

What does a man see by looking behind himself? He may seem to see nothing. What is that nothing? It is better than all the railroads and schoolhouses, the church steeples and factories; we can fasten our gaze upon. Why is this? Because it is the Substance out of which the genius of man is born. Its name has been called "Primal Dark." Jacob Boehme called it thus. But is nothingness, darkness, blankness, all that men can see by thus turning around to face his origin? By

---

[26] Greek mathematician & inventor, 287(?)-212 B.C. who documented the use of a lever and fulcrum and who made the word "Eureka!" part of our language, as he ran from his bath with the idea for how to tell the difference between lead and gold by seeing how much water they displace.

no manner of means. He shall find the whole Kingdom of Heaven. He shall find the true God. He shall find himself. He shall find the true nature of each one of his neighbors.

Seeing a neighbor's true nature cures that neighbor instantly. Who shall cure me of disease save him that sees no disease in me, but sees my true nature?

Spiritual Science is the orderly arrangement of Truth. It has for its particular effect the rapid hurrying of mind to the limit of its ability. What are you and what am I when we are hurried to the limit of our mental ability? We are at the door of the Kingdom of inspiration. What is inspiration? It is unaccountable wisdom.

The River of Jordan is called the God River. It is the Science of God as told by mind. As the River Jordan nears the Dead Sea, it falls rapidly. So the Science of God, as it nears the belt line of its limit, runs over that last device of mind to explain God, which we call Spiritual Science, with its twelve orderly statements of Truth. They are not new assertions, but they are the ultimates of religious reasonings as found in all Bibles. They hurry the mind to its limits so swiftly that you this minute have got as far as you can think. You do not wish to think. No evidence of being at the belt line where you can turn around and be your native self, inspiration itself, is better than a feeling of having reached the end of your thinking powers.

The Dead Sea has been found to contain the stuff for manufacturing every known article of commerce. So this nothing which we see as we turn around with our inner eyesight, is the origin of all that we have hoped for. As the Dead Sea has been maligned and misrepresented, so looking backward has been maligned. But looking forward has manufactured our present state of civilization, which is a miserable Failure.

The mission of Jesus was to call us as a race, to turn—to return. "If a man smite thee on the right cheek, turn to him the other also."

Here is a lesson in the return, the repent, the turn square around, principal. It means that if we are hit on our religious side with the strong knowledge that it is not a power to cure us so far as we have worked it up, we must look around to see and do everything different from what we have been seeing. As first and primarily, we have been seeing the outward world, we turn to see the world behind us. Thus we turn our very faith in outward forms, outward words, thoughts, around into the Divine Primal Dark. This faith is our left cheek. When both cheeks face the Primal State, we are faced square around.

Job was faced square around by supreme trouble. This was the smite on his religious cheek, which showed him that religion which was actually as good as the twelve lessons of Spiritual Science.

The first of these statements to the twelfth itself, Job makes:

There is only God.

That which is not God is nothing.

All is God. I am God.

I have the faith of God.

I work the works of God.

I understand God.

I see all things as born of God.

I see God plainly.

I sense the goodness of God in All.

There is but one world.

The wisdom of God faces me now.

To name God is to see God.

Put these cursory notes on the Spiritual Lessons beside Job's doctrine and see how they tally.
There is one passage of Job which we have not
had perfectly translated to match the truth lesson.
In the first arrangement of Spiritual Science at the
tenth lesson, there is a treatment for taking cogni-
zance of the perfection in this world of mankind;
seeing the perfect man in your worst foe; seeing
the perfect body in the most apparently diseased.

The present translation of Job's tenth lesson
reads: "I know that my Redeemer liveth and that

he shall stand at the latter day upon the earth."
[Job 19:25]

As it has been translated for another Bible, it reads: "For I know that He is eternal who is about to deliver me on earth, to restore this skin of mine which endures these things."

The first translation is orthodox religion, which puts health off into the next world. The second translation is the Spiritual Science which decrees everything to be done here on this earth, inside this, my skin. But neither one is the Dead Sea of the Absolute. By that sea, we see the Divine Nothing. We name it Jesus Christ. We keep our eyes fixed on it. Like the mathematician, Vieta, we watch it. Like him, we name it. He named what he was after. Are we after anything short of the Absolute?

Jesus Christ represents Absoluteness. "All power is given unto Me."

John watched till he saw those who kept this name given a new name. He saw them eat manna, that is, Absoluteness.

The earliest colleges for studying the presence of the Absolute were established by Samuel. But he did not originate them. He only restored them. Watching the Absolute, Elisha wrought miracles at the two schools of Gilgal and Jericho.

Whatever Elisha might have found out about the supreme kindness of looking behind him instead of outside of him, we are not told. But this you will find, namely, that there is no sorrow or death to follow your looking backward and letting what you name be brought forward. But there is always misery accompanying forcing your thought outward—Elisha's slaying his enemies; Peter's cutting off the servant's ear; John's asking for fire to destroy his neighbors.

If you fill a building with the Name of Jesus Christ, by the process of shooting the Name forward into that building, something will destroy the building, very likely, fire. If you look backward and name what sits on the throne, Jesus Christ, the divine power of Kindness, will shed itself over and through that building.

It is to the spreading forth of ideas outwardly that we owe all our civilization. But Jesus Christ said that His followers preached repentance and the Kingdom of Heaven would be visible. He did not admire civilization. When the Kingship of a great country was urged upon Him by the very people themselves, He declined it.

All that is brought to pass in your affairs, by your putting your words of will into your affairs, has a sting in it. But whatever comes from heaven while you look into it and name what you wish, has no sting.

As we look around us to "Him that sitteth on the throne," we ourselves are one with "Him that sitteth on the throne." The temple of God is our self. It is an opening body. We can disclose wonderful things. "The ark of His testament," said

John, was shown: The Shrine of His words and wills, which are not at all like our present words and wills, for they have no stings of poverty or death or disease.

Under the civilized wills of outward religions, statistics record great increases everywhere of sorrows.

Under the will of heaven into which we look straight, we shall not record a single death, nor notice a single hungry or disappointed or defeated one.

We do not need to use our will. We find a will divine that uses itself.

We do not need to use our thoughts. We find a lofty, noble thought using itself its own way. We rest from effort and yet wonderful works do follow us.

What man is so supernal in power and wisdom, as the man who has laid down his power and wisdom ?

What world is so beyond the pen to describe, as the world not made with hands of effort—the eternal world of many mansions where the Father-Mother makes divine man.

XII

FREE GRACE

"God said unto them, 'Be fruitful, and multiply and replenish the earth' ... And God saw everything that He had made and behold it was very good." [Genesis 1:28-31]

"And the seven angels which had the seven trumpets prepared themselves to sound." [Revelation 8:6]

"And there were voices, and thunderings, and an earthquake, and great hail." [Revelation 8:5]

"And they sing the song of Moses, the servant of God, and the song of the Lamb." [Revelation 15:3]

Here is the Fact. Something is Fact.

Some sing the song of Moses, and they call that which they sing The Fact.

Some sing the song of the Lamb, and they call that which they sing, Fact.

But John, the seer, found that in heaven they sing the two songs and they are not touched by death, pain, hardship, prisons, or debts.

Let it be known that the Song of Moses is Scientific Truth—that is, Truth which can be reasoned from some premise and proved in some external appearance.

And let it be known that the Song of the Lamb is the Unaccountable Fact which was before Truth. There had to be something for Truth to be about. And that Something which Truth mentions is the Unaccountable, The Fact.

Whoever watches an ant will have peculiar experiences. His brain cells will open and small shining particles will suddenly appear in them. These particles will clash together and he will know new things or particles or machinery. Whoever watches a white lily will find peculiar changes transpiring in his clothing. Whoever watches birds will find peculiar changes coming to his house and bread.

"For what thou seest, man. That, too, become thou must; God, if thou seest God, Dust, if thou seest dust."

Now, if we watch the Song of Science, we are forever transposing. That is, we have laws of thought, laws of speech, laws of actions. If we speak, we are careful of our words, lest they turn our hair white or give us rheumatism. If we meditate, we are careful to have no prejudices, lest we find our property lost and our children vicious. This is transposition. That is, something here transposes itself into something there. It is sure that we can, by transposition or law, get rid of nothing. We simply shift it from one side to another.

I borrow $10 of you, and you get afraid I will not pay you, so you dun me on a day when I cannot pay. It will not make any difference how many years after this Transaction Science permits you to flourish, but as sure as you are now traveling on the circumference of a circle, you will come to a day when someone will dun you for what you cannot pay. This is transposition. This is the Song of Moses. This is Science.

The Song of Science has the principle of denial. It tells you that if you deny that as a divine being you could be dunned because as Spirit you never dunned, you will go scot free of duns. But this science also adds that you have to be particular to state what part of dunning you put out of your circle, or you will find that when the sun duns your eyes to shine, they will not shine, and when and where the voices of your loved ones dun you to hear them, you cannot hear. Thus accurate and exact is this science.

It is transposition of word and thought into outwardly visible things, and reaction of the outwardly visible on thoughts and words. Even supposing thoughts and words are left through denial *in toto* of matter, then there is the misty realm between matter and thought which was and is a transposition of thoughts and words into another stuff than matter.

The Song of transposition is the song of the law. It sings of the power of the word. It makes the ramifications and transpositions of words an endless song. Yet we may be telling the truth about every motion.

This will forever be the song of the law-the Song of Moses. It is Truth as related to phenomena, but it is the Truth of the accountable.

The Song of the Lamb is the song of the Unaccountable. To the religious mind, it is a stumbling block. Why? Because "I will have mercy upon whom I will have mercy; and whom I will. I harden."

It is to reason, foolishness. Why? Because there is no law or responsibility in it.

When the Unaccountable is sung, it creates astonishments. It is the Song of the Lamb. It tells of heaven. It causes the law to bend down low, as a back for the Kingdom of Heaven to walk downward into earth with.

Put the Song of Transposition going. Keep it going. The more you work it, the sooner you see the need of another song. This is the Lamb, the Unlawed, the Unaccountable.

Now keep your eye on the Unaccountable, and you yourself will be the Unaccountable. But there is something to be sung about the Unlawed. What is it? It is that which has no reasoning, or Greekism. It is that which has no religion, or Jewism. It is represented in the universe as Jesus Christ.

With this Name opened to man, the seven angels prepare to sound.

There is the stumbling-block Fact in the universe-Jesus Christ. Sing what it is that is not according to law or reason.

There is the foolishness Fact in the universe. Sing what it is that is foolishness.

The utmost of foolishness is the Jesus Christ Fact in the universe. Put this song with the song of transposition and we have no use for the law, yet we understand the law. This is heaven. Heaven is here.

The Song of the Lamb that God saw as good, touches all who are singing the song of transposition.

Remember Jesus Christ is the Fact, not accounted for—The Lamb.

Jesus Christ suffered death once for all men. Whoever looks to that Fact, goes scot free of death. Have you looked at that Fact? Then you will never die "But," you say, "good Christians

die." Do they? "Well," you say, "they seem to die."
Do Christians singing the song of the Fact die?
No. They take the Unaccountable Fact and say
unto It, or Him, or Her, "I take thee at Thy word.
As thou didst die once for me, I need not die." This
is actual Christianity. Artificial Christianity says,
"If Jesus died, why should I not die?" "If Jesus
suffered, how cowardly I am to complain of suffer-
ing."

Let this 12th lesson teach you the good Song
of the Lamb—the Unaccountable Fact.

Look unto Him that sitteth on the throne
within your own Self—up-look high—and sing this
Song:

> Thou didst take hardship once for me. and I do not
> have to take hardship. I go scot free.

> Thou didst take sickness once for me. and I do not
> need to take sickness. I go scot free.

> Thou didst take debts once for me, and I do not need
> to owe debts. I go scot free.

> Thou didst take shame and disgrace once for me,
> and I need not take shame and disgrace. I go scot free.

> Thou didst take bravery once for me, and now I do
> not have to be brave. I go scot free.

> Thou didst take pain once for me, and I do not have
> to bear pain. I go scot free.

> Thou didst bear me once as a burden, and now no
> one has to bear me as a burden. They go scot free.

On whatever line or plan of life or experience we are grinding out our existence, this Song of the Unaccountable is the Song of the Lamb.

"Behold the Lamb of God that taketh away the sin of the world."

Do you see any reason why any Being or Fact should take your sins, your debts your pains, your disgrace, your poverty, your shirking, your bravery, and you go scot free?

This is the Unlawed. There is no law for the Lamb; no reasoning about the Lamb; no transposition from right to left.

The 24 elders fall down. The throne is visible.

The song of the law is that I must meet death when it shoots its threats at me, with my guns of scientific denials of death. I must work my mental guns on the physical battalions of death. But the Song of the Lamb is that I may look at the Fact in the Universe, the One that took death once for me, leaving me free from death.

How long might mankind fight death? As long as he pleases. As long as he shall sing Moses. Five thousand years, if he pleases; ten million years, if he likes. But the Fact remains that death is self-imposed, or self-accepted. Man, by looking at the deathless Fact, goes scot free of sin, of poverty, of pain, of hardships, of disgrace, of hurts. The Eternal and Absolute Fact is the Origin of the Transposition of words into things and things into words, for it is by the Fact that the phenomenon of turning over and over keeps up.

The 12th stone is the amethyst, free peace, free prosperity, free health, free life, free wisdom.

Glory be to the Lamb. Glory be to the Fact. To Thee I look. Thee, I receive. Thou hast received all that I have, and I am free.

Thou bearest my burdens—I bear none.

Thou takest my death—I die not.

Thou takest my shame.

I see the Fact and am One with it.

Ω

Notes

Notes

Other Books by Emma Curtis Hopkins

- Class Lessons of 1888 (WiseWoman Press)
- Bible Interpretations
- Esoteric Philosophy in Spiritual Science
- Genesis Series
- High Mysticism
- Gospel Series (WiseWoman Press)
- Resume (WiseWoman Press)
- Scientific Christian Mental Practice (DeVorss)

Books about Emma Curtis Hopkins & her teachings

- Emma Curtis Hopkins, Forgotten Founder of New Thought – Gail Harley
- Unveiling Your Hidden Power: Emma Curtis Hopkins' Metaphysics for the 21st Century (also as a Workbook and as A Guide for Teachers) – Ruth L. Miller

To find more of Emma's work, including some previously unpublished material, log on to:

www.emmacurtishopkins.org

WISEWOMAN PRESS
1521 NE Jantzen Ave #143
Portland, Oregon 97217
800.603.3005
www.wisewomanpress.com

by Emma Curtis Hopkins

Resume

Gospel Series

Class Lessons of 1888

Self Treatments

by Ruth L. Miller

Uncommon Prayer

Notre Dame: Mary Magdalene & the Divine Feminine

150 Years of Healing: The Founders and Science of New Thought

Unveiling Your Hidden Power: Emma Curtis Hopkins' Metaphysics for the 21st Century

**Watch our website for release dates
and order information!**
www.wisewomanpress.com